THE HEALING POWER OF BOUNDARIES:

Love, Faith, and Truth

Without Losing Yourself

Dr. Jean Héder Petit-Frère

The Healing Power of Boundaries

Love, Faith, and Truth Without Losing Yourself

Copyright © 2025 by Dr. Jean Héder Petit-Frère

All rights reserved.
No part of this publication may be reproduced, stored in a retrieval system, or transmitted in any form or by any means—electronic, mechanical, photocopying, recording, or otherwise—without the prior written permission of the author, except in the case of brief quotations embodied in critical articles or reviews.

All Scripture quotations, unless otherwise indicated, are taken from the New King James Version®, copyright © 1982 by Thomas Nelson. Used by permission. All rights reserved.

Edited and compiled in collaboration with:
Jean Héder Petit-Frère International

ISBN (Paperback): 978-1-7353215-7-8

For more resources, teachings, and Kingdom training,
visit: www.jhpetitfrere.com

All rights reserved worldwide.

Table of Content

Dedication	11
Acknowledgements	13
Foreword	15
Embracing the Journey: A Testament of Faith, Pain, and Triumph	15
Introduction	19
Why This Book Had to Be Written	19
Who This Book Is For	20
A Word About the Journey Ahead	21
Chapter One	22
Boundaries and Responsibility	23
Identity, and True Unity	23
Identity Before Limits	23
Unity Is Not Fusion	24
What Boundaries Do—and What They Do Not	25
Why Boundaries Feel Threatening	25
Love, Limits, and Wisdom	25
The Foundation Moving Forward	26
Reflection	27
Prayer	27
Summary	27
Chapter Two	30
Why Love Alone Is Not Enough	31
When Love Carries What Boundaries Were Meant to Hold	31
The Burden We Place on Love	32
When Staying Becomes Proof of Virtue	32
Love Cannot Replace Responsibility	34
Why Good Intentions Are Not Enough	34
The Cost of Boundaryless Love	35
A Necessary Reframe	36
What This Means Going Forward	36
Reflection	37

Prayer	37
Summary	37
Chapter Three	38
The Damage Boundaries Are Meant to Prevent	39
How Quiet Compromises Erode Safety	39
The Slow Disappearance of the Self	39
When Faith Becomes a Silencer	40
Love Without Safety	40
Identity Erosion in Long Marriages	41
The Body Remembers What the Mouth Cannot Say	42
What Children Learn Without Being Told	42
The Comfort of False Peace	43
The Accumulation Effect	44
A Necessary Clarification	44
An Invitation, Not an Accusation	44
Reflection	45
Prayer	45
Summary	45
Chapter Four	48
Why Boundaries Are So Hard to Establish in Marriage	49
Why Clarity Feels Dangerous Before It Feels Healing	49
The Power of Hope in the Early Years	49
Faith That Becomes Conflicted	50
Fear of What Boundaries Might Cost	51
Power Imbalances That Raise the Stakes	52
Trauma and the Habit of Adaptation	53
The Shock of Waking Up Late	53
Boundaries Change the Relationship	54
A Necessary Reframe	55
Reflection	55
Prayer	55
Summary	56
Chapter Five	58

How to Set Boundaries Without Turning Love Into War	59
Clarity Without Conflict	59
Boundaries Begin Inside, Not in Conversation	59
The Difference Between Naming a Boundary and Attacking a Person	60
Speaking Without Threatening	60
Why Specificity Matters	61
Timing and Tone Matter More Than Perfect Words	61
Expect Discomfort—and Do Not Misinterpret It	62
Boundaries Are Not Negotiations	62
The Role of Consequences	63
When Guilt Appears	63
A Gentle Truth	63
Reflection	64
Prayer	64
Summary	64
Chapter Six	66
What Healthy Boundaries Sound Like in Real Life	67
Putting Words to Wisdom	67
When Emotions Begin to Overwhelm the Relationship	67
When Time and Energy Are Being Drained	68
When Forgiveness Is Confused With Immediate Trust	69
When Family of Origin Begins to Intrude	70
When Finances Become a Source of Tension or Control	71
When Sexual Intimacy Requires Safety and Consent	71
When Faith Is Used to Avoid Necessary Conversations	72
A Final Word on Tone and Timing	72
Reflection	73
Prayer	74
Summary	74
Chapter Seven	76
Enforcing Boundaries When They Are Tested	77
Holding the Line	77

Why Boundaries Are Tested	77
The Difference Between Explaining and Enforcing	78
What Enforcement Actually Looks Like	78
Staying Calm When Emotions Rise	79
When Guilt Tries to Undo Progress	79
Recognizing Emotional Pushback	80
The Line Between Discomfort and Harm	80
When Boundaries Are Repeatedly Ignored	80
What Enforcement Reveals	81
Choosing Integrity Over Illusion	82
Reflection	82
Prayer	82
Summary	82
Chapter Eight	84
When Boundaries Were Never in Place	85
Late Awareness, Lasting Change:	85
Repairing, Resetting, or Redefining the Relationship	85
When the Past Cannot Be Rewritten	86
Grieving What Was Lost—Without Staying There	86
The Reset Conversation	87
The Season of Recalibration	87
When Repair Is Possible	88
When Reset Meets Resistance	88
Redefining the Relationship	89
Children and Late Boundary Work	89
Choosing Integrity Over Regret	89
Reflection	90
Prayer	90
Summary	90
Chapter Nine	92
Love, Forgiveness, and the Courage to Set Limits	93
Love With Wisdom	93
Forgiveness Heals the Heart, Not the Pattern	93

Grace Does Not Cancel Accountability	94
What Scripture Means When It Says Love "Endures All Things"	95
What Love Bears—and What It Does Not	95
Forgiveness Is Not the Same as Relational Continuity	96
Endurance Is Not Self-Erasure	96
Jesus as the Model of Bounded Love	97
Love That Cannot Say No Is Not Love—It Is Fear	98
A Redemptive Reframe	98
Where This Leads	98
Reflection	99
Prayer	99
Summary	99
Chapter Ten	100
When Boundaries Are Violated and Hard Decisions Must Be Faced	101
When Words Fail and Reality Must Be Faced"	101
When a Violation Becomes a Pattern	101
The Subtle Erosion of Discernment	102
Manipulation Wears Many Faces	102
Escalation Is Not Cruelty	103
The Difference Between Hope and Denial	104
When Staying Requires Self-Abandonment	105
Hard Decisions Are Not Hasty Decisions	105
Living Without Illusion	105
A Word for the Crossroads	106
Reflection	106
Prayer	106
Summary	107
Chapter Eleven	108
Discernment, Counsel, and the Wisdom of Not Walking Alone	109
Finding Clarity Through Community	109
Why Discernment Needs Perspective	109
The Danger of Isolation	110

Not All Advice Is Equal	110
Choosing the Right Voices	111
The Role of Professional Support	111
Pastoral Care and Spiritual Covering	112
Accountability Changes the Dynamic	112
When Community Becomes Pressure	113
Integrating Faith, Wisdom, and Reality	113
A Steadying Truth	113
Reflection	114
Prayer	114
Summary	114
Chapter Twelve	116
Living With Boundaries:	117
Freedom, Peace, and a New Way of Relating	117
The Quiet That Returns Inside	117
Love Feels Lighter	117
Intimacy Grows Where Safety Exists	118
The End of Emotional Over functioning	118
Marriage Becomes a Choice Again	119
Not Every Relationship Looks the Same on the Other Side	119
You Become Someone You Trust	119
Faith Finds Its Balance	120
The Beginning of Peace	120
Reflection	121
Prayer	121
Summary	121
Chapter Thirteen	122
Where Boundaries Touch Real Life	123
The Places We Were Never Taught to Look	123
Emotional Life	123
Communication	124
Time and Energy	125
Sexual Life	126

Finances	128
Family of Origin (Past)	129
Family of Origin (Present)	130
Spiritual Life	132
Spiritual Altars and Generational Patterns	133
A Deep Integration	135
Reflection	135
Prayer	136
Summary	136
APPENDIX A — A THEOLOGY DETOX	**139**
When Scripture Is Honored in Its Intention, Not Merely Quoted	139
1. "Love Bears All Things"	139
Why This Verse Is Often Misunderstood	140
Biblical Clarification	140
Lived Application	140
Applied correction:	140
2. Forgiveness	141
Why This Confusion Is Common	141
Biblical Clarification	141
Lived Application	141
Applied correction:	141
3. Faith	142
Why This Distortion Develops	142
Biblical Clarification	142
Lived Application	142
Applied correction:	142
4. Submission	143
Why This Teaching Has Caused Pain	143
Biblical Clarification	143
Lived Application	143
Applied correction:	143
5. Headship and Authority	144
Why This Misunderstanding Persists	144

Biblical Clarification	144
Lived Application	144
Applied correction:	144
6. Suffering	144
Why This Interpretation Is Tempting	145
Biblical Clarification	145
Lived Application	145
Applied correction:	145
Why Silence Feels Faithful	146
Biblical Clarification	146
Lived Application	146
Applied correction:	146
Final Detox Declaration	146
Conclusion	148
Living Whole, Loving Well	148
AUTHOR BIO	151

Dedication

This book is dedicated to those who have loved with sincerity, believed with conviction, and remained faithful through seasons of confusion—yet quietly felt themselves shrinking in the process.

It is for those who stayed longer than they understood, endured more than was required, and spiritualized pain because they believed love demanded it. For those who were taught to carry burdens in silence, to equate endurance with holiness, and to confuse faithfulness with self-erasure.

This book is also for couples and individuals who desire something better—not a love that merely survives, but one that is honest, whole, and life-giving. A love that can withstand truth. A faith that does not fear wisdom. A commitment that does not require the loss of one's identity.

May these pages serve as permission to pause, to reflect, and to realign.

May they remind you that God never asked you to disappear in order to prove your devotion.

And may you rediscover the freedom to love deeply, believe wisely, and live fully—without losing yourself.

Acknowledgements

This book represents far more than a writing project; it is the fruit of years of ministry, reflection, personal struggle, prayer, and growth. It was shaped in conversations, in quiet moments of reckoning, and in the sacred tension between what I believed and what I lived.

I wish to express my deepest gratitude to my spiritual mother, Dr. Pat Morgan, whose life, wisdom, and uncompromising commitment to truth have profoundly influenced my walk with God and my understanding of leadership. Her voice has consistently called me to integrity—of heart, of doctrine, and of life. To have her write the foreword to this book is both an honor and a sacred trust.

I am also grateful to the many pastors, leaders, counselors, and believers across cultures and nations who entrusted me with their stories. Your courage to speak honestly about love, faith, marriage, and pain revealed a shared struggle that demanded a compassionate and truthful response. This book carries echoes of your voices.

To my family, whose patience and grace have accompanied this journey: thank you for walking with me through seasons of learning and unlearning. The lessons contained in these pages were not formed in isolation but in the lived reality of relationships that required humility, repentance, growth, and renewed understanding.

Above all, I acknowledge God, whose truth heals without shaming and whose grace never contradicts wisdom. This work is offered as an act of stewardship—to honor His Word, protect His people, and restore balance where misunderstanding has caused harm.

Foreword

Embracing the Journey: A Testament of Faith, Pain, and Triumph

IN THE TAPESTRY OF HUMAN experience, there are moments when the soul is called to wrestle with questions that transcend the boundaries of reason, faith, and tradition. This work emerges from such a place—a heartfelt quest that dares to respond openly to the deepest cries of the heart, the longing for purpose, and the relentless pursuit of hope amidst suffering. It is written not only for the broken-hearted or those navigating the stormy seas of despair, but also for the seekers of truth, for believers and non-believers alike. All are touched by the universal realities of pain, confusion, resilience, and the longing for restoration.

Through these pages, you will witness an honest exploration of the intricate interplay between faith and suffering. The journey described here is one marked by moments of intense spiritual anguish, as well as bursts of laughter and defiant hope. The author's story is woven into the wider narrative of a people striving to build, to heal, and to overcome. From the cries of the people of Ayiti—Haiti—to the bold efforts made to serve, restore, and uplift others, the account is both personal and communal. It honors the spiritual legacy of mentors and forebearers, celebrating the wisdom inherited from those who have walked before, and acknowledging the unfinished work that continues to call forth new generations to lead and to serve.

As you turn these pages, you'll encounter a voice that has been tempered by suffering and shaped by relentless opposition, yet never silenced by defeat. The author stands as a witness to divine grace—a testament to the enduring faith that grows stronger in adversity. Through spiritual battles, moments of shame, and the refining fire of singlehood and leadership, a new sense of purpose and blessing is revealed. The narrative moves beyond personal pain to encompass the broader vision of kingdom building, urging readers to rise above the limitations imposed by history, circumstance, and human frailty.

This foreword invites you to journey alongside a servant who has learned to rest on the high places of faith, whose hopes have been forged in the crucible of struggle, and whose vision extends to building altars of significance for generations yet to come. It is a call to embrace the blessings and responsibilities of legacy, and to recognize the divine appointment to speak truth, extend mercy, and foster renewal in lands and hearts longing for transformation. May you find, within these words, not only an account of pain and bravery, but also an invitation to participate in the wondrous work of restoration, faith, and inheritance. For as we are reminded—"I am yours. And you are Mine. And all is well." Let this journey inspire you to seek, to believe, and to build anew.

Dr Pat Morgan (Ph.D)
Frmr Prof. ORU, CGST, and CNC.
Educational Psychologist, Author.

Introduction

Why This Book Had to Be Written

There are many marriages that look intact from the outside and feel fractured on the inside. They have survived years, sometimes decades. They have endured seasons of difficulty, disappointment, misunderstanding, and silence. They have not ended—but neither have they flourished.

I have sat with people who did everything they were told a good spouse should do. They stayed. They prayed. They forgave. They tried harder. They adjusted. They absorbed. And yet, somewhere along the way, they lost themselves.

They did not stop loving.
They stopped being present.

This book was not born out of theory. It emerged from conversations—quiet ones, often held behind closed doors—where faithful men and women finally found words for what they had been living. Questions surfaced again and again, sometimes whispered, sometimes asked with tears:

Is it wrong to want limits?
Does love require silence?
Why does forgiveness keep reopening the same wound?
Is endurance the same as faithfulness?

For many, the struggle was not a lack of commitment. It was the absence of structure. Love existed. Covenant existed. But boundaries did not.

And love, when left without structure, eventually becomes heavy.

This book is not written to dismantle marriage. It is written to rescue it from the quiet erosion that occurs when truth is postponed and limits are never named. It challenges the idea that longevity alone is evidence of health, and it confronts the belief that suffering automatically sanctifies a relationship.

Marriage was never meant to require the disappearance of one person so that another could remain comfortable.

This is a book about learning how to love without disappearing, forgive without enabling, and remain committed without betraying oneself.

It is written for those who want their marriages not just to last, but to breathe.

Who This Book Is For

This book is for couples who sense that something is off but cannot quite name it. It is for individuals who have awakened late to patterns they once normalized. It is for believers who love God deeply yet feel torn between faith and self-respect. It is for pastors, counselors, and leaders who want language that heals without excusing harm.

It is not a book of quick solutions or simplistic answers. It is an invitation to clarity.

You will not find condemnation here. But you will find truth. And truth, while sometimes uncomfortable, is always kinder than illusion.

INTRODUCTION

A Word About the Journey Ahead

What you are about to read may unsettle long-held assumptions. It may challenge familiar spiritual language. It may invite you to grieve what was lost and reconsider what is possible.

That is intentional.

Boundaries are not about control. They are about stewardship—of the self, of love, and of the covenant entrusted to you. And stewardship always begins with honesty.

If you are willing to engage that honesty, this book will walk with you—carefully, firmly, compassionately—toward a healthier way of relating.

CHAPTER ONE

Boundaries and Responsibility

Identity, and True Unity

At the heart of every boundary is responsibility. Healthy relationships require clarity about what belongs to whom—emotionally, spiritually, and behaviorally.

Marriage does not erase personal responsibility. Covenant does not dissolve agency. Two people do not become one by losing themselves in each other but by choosing partnership as whole, differentiated individuals.

Boundaries serve as the structure for navigating this challenging balance between individuality and partnership.

When responsibility is unclear, one person often begins to over function while the other under functions. One adapts, absorbs, and compensates. The other grows accustomed to unchecked access. Over time, imbalance becomes normal—and resentment quietly accumulates.

Boundaries interrupt this pattern. They restore ownership. They return adults to themselves.

Identity Before Limits

People who struggle most with boundaries are rarely unloving. They are often deeply caring, empathetic, and committed. What they lack is not compassion, it is clarity of self.

When someone does not know what they value, what they need, or what they can no longer tolerate, boundaries feel confusing or selfish.

Saying no feels wrong. Speaking up feels disloyal.

This is why so many people in long marriages eventually confess, "I don't even know who I am anymore."

Marriage did not require that loss. Boundarylessness allowed it.

Having a clear understanding of one's identity does not pose a threat to unity; instead, it serves as the foundation for building healthy relationships. With a solid grasp of their identity, values, and needs for personal growth, individuals can establish boundaries that safeguard their well-being and foster meaningful relationships. When individuals make self-awareness and self-care a priority, they can craft a life that is genuine and enriching for themselves and those in their circle. Viewing boundaries not as obstacles to intimacy but as vital instruments for sustaining healthy and harmonious relationships. It is the foundation of it.

Unity Is Not Fusion

There is a form of togetherness that looks spiritual but is deeply unhealthy. In this kind of fusion, disagreement feels like betrayal. Silence becomes the price of peace. One person shrinks so that the relationship can survive while the other dominates.

This is not biblical unity.

True unity allows difference. It permits a voice. It creates space for honesty without fear of abandonment. Fusion, by contrast, demands sameness and punishes distinction.

Boundaries protect unity from becoming emotional suffocation.

What Boundaries Do—and What They Do Not

Boundaries do not exist to control another person. They do not force change or guarantee agreement. What they do is clarify reality.

They define what behavior you will participate in and what you will not. They establish consequences that protect dignity and emotional safety. They replace unspoken expectations with visible truth.

A boundary does not say, *"You must change."*
It says, *"If this continues, I will change how I participate."*

That distinction is critical. It preserves freedom on both sides while refusing self-betrayal.

Why Boundaries Feel Threatening

Boundaries often feel threatening—not because they are wrong, but because they disrupt familiar dynamics. They challenge patterns that benefited from silence. They introduce accountability where there was once unchecked access.

For some, this discomfort is interpreted as unloving. In reality, it is simply unfamiliar.

Boundaries do not create conflict. They reveal it.

Love, Limits, and Wisdom

Jesus loved deeply, yet He lived with clear limits. He withdrew from crowds. He confronted misuse of power. He refused manipulation. He did not give unrestricted access to everyone who wanted it.

Love without limits was never His model.

Boundaries are not a failure of love. They are an expression of wisdom. Proverbs 4:7 (NKJV):"Wisdom is the principal thing; therefore get wisdom. And in all your getting, get understanding.

The Foundation Moving Forward

Everything in this book rests on one essential truth: love needs structure in order to remain life-giving and healthy in relationships. Without boundaries, love can become suffocating and enabling. By setting clear limits and boundaries, we are able to show respect for ourselves and others, deepening our relationships. Just as Jesus demonstrated, boundaries are an important aspect of love and wisdom in our lives. Love with limits is not only possible but also necessary for true and lasting connection.

Forgiveness needs boundaries to remain redemptive. Covenant needs truth to remain alive.

Without boundaries, marriage becomes endurance.
With boundaries, marriage becomes a choice.
Without boundaries, marriage can become toxic and destructive.
With boundaries, marriage becomes a safe and healthy space for growth and intimacy.

Real love begins with a free and honestly renewed choice. Boundaries in relationships allow for respect, trust, and growth to thrive. They create a safe space for individuals to express themselves, communicate openly, and address difficulties as a team.

Without boundaries, relationships can become overwhelming, enabling unhealthy patterns to persist. By setting and respecting boundaries, we show love not only for ourselves but also for our partners, building a strong and meaningful bond built on mutual understanding and respect.

Reflection

Take a moment to consider how you have understood boundaries until now. Were they something you associated with distance, rejection, or conflict? Or were they simply absent—never named, never modeled, never discussed?

Ask yourself gently: Where in my marriage have responsibility and identity become blurred? Where have I adapted instead of clarified?

Boundaries begin with awareness, not action. There is no need to judge what you are noticing—only to name it honestly.

Prayer

God of truth and wisdom, Help me see clearly where I have lost myself in the name of love. Teach me the difference between unity and disappearance. Give me courage to honor the self You entrusted to me and wisdom to love without abandoning truth. Amen.

Summary

> Setting emotional, spiritual, and behavioral limits for each partner is essential for a healthy marriage and is a key part of being responsible for your actions. A happy marriage does not require people to lose their individuality. Instead, real togetherness happens when two whole, separate people choose to work together without giving up their sense of self. On the other hand, not having limits can lead to an imbalance where one partner takes on too much responsibility and the other does not do

enough, which can lead to anger and a loss of self-esteem.

The idea behind this chapter is that people often have trouble setting limits not because they do not love themselves enough, but because they do not have a clear sense of who they are, and they confuse real connection with harmful entanglement. In this situation, boundaries do not control other people or force them to change. Instead, they define reality, protect personal freedom, and keep people from hurting themselves. As a result, the chapter comes to the conclusion that love needs limits to stay alive, and that boundaries help marriage grow from just sticking together to a conscious, healthy commitment based on understanding, honesty, and mutual respect.

BOUNDARIES AND RESPONSIBILITY

CHAPTER TWO

Why Love Alone Is Not Enough

When Love Carries What Boundaries Were Meant to Hold

Most people enter marriage believing that love will be sufficient. They assume that if affection is real, commitment sincere, and intentions good, everything else will eventually fall into place. And for a while, that belief seems justified. Love carries energy. It fuels patience. It softens disappointment. It creates hope.

But over time, many couples discover something unsettling: love can be present, sincere, and even deep, yet the relationship still becomes heavy.

It becomes burdened with unmet expectations, unresolved conflicts, and unspoken resentments. Love alone is not enough to sustain a healthy and thriving relationship. It demands more than mere affection and good intentions alone. It necessitates open communication, mutual consent, and a shared commitment to overcoming obstacles together. Love may serve as the foundation, but it is not the sole essential component required for a successful partnership. For a relationship to flourish, couples need to be ready to put in the necessary effort and dedication to strengthen their bond and ensure its long-term success.

When a relationship becomes strained, feelings of guilt often arise. People hesitate to name their dissatisfaction because they know they love their spouse. They stay quiet because they assume something must be wrong with them. After all, isn't love supposed to conquer everything?

This assumption has quietly damaged countless marriages.

Love is essential. But love, on its own, is not enough to sustain a healthy relationship over time.

The Burden We Place on Love

When boundaries are absent, love is asked to do too much. It becomes responsible for regulating behavior, absorbing disappointment, managing emotional fallout, and maintaining peace—all at once.

Love becomes a substitute for structure.
Love becomes a burden.
Love becomes work.

In these marriages, love is expected to:

- endure repeated hurt without protection
- forgive without safeguards
- remain warm in emotionally unsafe conditions
- compensate for a lack of accountability

Eventually, love grows tired—not because it is weak, but because it was never meant to function alone.

Love is powerful, but it is not structural. Without boundaries, it bends under pressure.

When Staying Becomes Proof of Virtue

In many long-term marriages, endurance is mistaken for health. Couples point to the number of years they have stayed together as evidence that things must be fine. Ask yourself this question. Is everything alright when nobody is looking? Yet longevity does not always reflect wholeness.

People stay for many reasons:

- shared history
- children
- finances
- fear of change
- religious pressure
- emotional dependence

None of these automatically indicate intimacy, safety, or mutual respect.

Some marriages survive while quietly hollowing out. Conversations become practical. Emotions are managed rather than shared. Conflict is avoided not because it has been resolved, but because it feels too dangerous to address. However, true connection and fulfillment cannot be sustained through mere appearances and longevity. It requires genuine communication, vulnerability, and a deep sense of understanding between partners.

Love remains—but it is constrained, muted, and often lonely. Love endures on the inside but is unable to make a complete connection, be shared, or find companionship due to factors such as fear, unspoken boundaries, or difficult circumstances. Without open communication and vulnerability, love can become stagnant and unfulfilling.

The Illusion of Peace

One of the most deceptive outcomes of boundaryless love is the appearance of peace. In relationships influenced by boundaryless love, there may be fewer arguments. Less overt conflict. More predictability.

However, this peace is often achieved by maintaining silence.

If one spouse consistently adjusts to prevent tension, the relationship may appear calmer on the surface but grow more distant underneath. Unspoken frustration accumulates. Needs go unmet. Resentment finds subtle outlets.

This is not peace. It is containment.

True peace does not come from avoiding truth. It comes from making space for it.

John 8:31-32 NKJV—"Then Jesus said to those Jews who believed Him, 'If you abide in My word, you are My disciples indeed. And you shall know the truth, and the truth shall make you free."

Love Cannot Replace Responsibility

A relationship without boundaries slowly shifts responsibility onto the more accommodating partner. That person learns to anticipate moods, smooth over disruptions, and absorb emotional impact. Over time, they become the emotional regulator for the relationship.

The other partner may not be malicious. They may simply grow accustomed to unchecked access.

Lack of love is not what keeps this imbalance in place. It is sustained by a lack of limits.

Love cannot correct irresponsibility. Only boundaries can do that.

Why Good Intentions Are Not Enough

Many couples remain stuck because both partners mean well. There is no obvious villain. No dramatic betrayal. Just patterns that repeat, unresolved and unaddressed.

Apologies are offered. Promises are made. Yet nothing fundamentally changes.

This is where many people become confused. They ask, "If the intention is good, why does this still hurt?"

Because intention does not replace impact. And sincerity does not eliminate consequence.

Boundaries translate intention into behavior. Without them, love remains aspirational rather than transformational.

The Cost of Boundaryless Love

Over time, love without boundaries comes with a price.

The price is paid in:

- emotional fatigue
- diminished self-respect
- quiet resentment
- loss of desire
- spiritual confusion

People begin to question themselves. They wonder why they feel distant or numb despite their commitment. They pray harder, try longer, and blame themselves more deeply.

But the issue is not a lack of devotion.

It is the absence of structure.

When there aren't any clear rules or structures in a relationship that spell out roles, responsibilities, and standards, this is called "absence of structure." Devotion has no clear base if it lacks order. Love turns into self-neglect instead of caring, effort turns into impulsiveness instead of planning, and faith becomes a way to stay strong instead of a way to find your way. People stay dedicated, but they don't know what their responsibilities are, what others' responsibilities are, or how boundaries are supposed to protect, not punish.

A Necessary Reframe

Love is not meant to replace truth.
Forgiveness is not meant to cancel limits.
Commitment is not meant to erase selfhood.

Love flourishes where boundaries exist—not because boundaries restrict love, but because they protect it from collapse.

Love becomes lighter when boundaries support it. Safer. More resilient.

When love is forced to function alone, it eventually becomes a burden.

What This Means Going Forward

If love alone has not healed what hurts, it is not because you failed. It is because love was asked to do what boundaries were meant to do.

This realization is not discouraging. It is liberating.

Because what love cannot accomplish by endurance, boundaries can accomplish by clarity. And clarity, once embraced, changes everything.

Reflection

Love has carried much in your relationship. Perhaps it has carried more than it should have. Consider where love has been asked to compensate for missing structure, accountability, or honesty.

Ask yourself: What has love been carrying that the boundaries were meant to hold? This reflection is not about diminishing love—but about relieving it of impossible burdens.

Prayer

God of love, Release me from the belief that enduring everything is the same as loving well. Show me how to support love with truth so that what I give is life-giving, not self-erasing. Amen.

Summary

> At first, love gives you energy and hope, but over time, relationships can suffer from failed expectations, problems that are not solved, and anger that is not spoken. A lot of the time, couples expect love to take on too much, which can make them emotionally tired and hurt their relationships. True happiness and closeness rely on being able to talk to each other, respect each other's space, and set clear limits. This keeps love from becoming a burden. The chapter makes the point that goals alone, no matter how good, cannot replace the accountability that boundaries offer. In the end, it says that structure and duty are necessary for love to grow, which makes you think about how you and your partner can free love from unnecessary burdens.

CHAPTER THREE

The Damage Boundaries Are Meant to Prevent

How Quiet Compromises Erode Safety

Most damage in marriage does not arrive suddenly. It accumulates quietly, almost politely, through small concessions that seem harmless at first. A conversation avoided. A feeling swallowed. A line crossed and quickly excused. Over time, what began as patience slowly becomes self-erasure.

This is why the absence of boundaries is so difficult to detect early. The relationship does not collapse—it adapts. And adaptation, when unexamined, can feel like maturity.

But adaptation without limits carries a cost.

The Slow Disappearance of the Self

One of the earliest signs of boundary damage is internal confusion. People begin to lose clarity about what they feel, what they need, and what they want. Not because those things disappeared, but because expressing them proved inconvenient, risky, or disruptive.

In many marriages, one partner learns—subtly—that honesty leads to tension, withdrawal, or conflict. Over time, silence becomes the safer option. Needs are minimized. Discomfort is rationalized. Emotional expression is delayed indefinitely.

Eventually, people say things like, "I don't even know what I feel anymore." This is not emotional maturity. It is emotional survival.

Boundaries protect the self from being slowly edited out of the relationship.

When Faith Becomes a Silencer

In spiritually committed marriages, boundary damage often hides behind religious language. Endurance is praised. Sacrifice is spiritualized. Suffering is framed as virtue.

People begin to wonder whether their pain is a sign of weakness rather than a signal of harm. Some people begin to believe they have done something wrong or that there is something wrong with them. When this is combined with rejection, it can gradually develop into self-blame and even self-hatred if not handled. They ask themselves if wanting change means they lack faith, patience, or humility.

This confusion is deeply damaging.

Faith was never meant to mute conscience or override wisdom. When spiritual language is used to discourage honest confrontation, the result is not holiness—it is internal fracture.

Boundaries protect faith from being weaponized against the soul.

Love Without Safety

Love is meant to feel safe. Not perfect—but safe enough, to be honest and open.

When boundaries are absent, safety erodes. Conversations feel unpredictable. Emotional responses feel disproportionate. Apologies come without lasting change. Promises are offered, then quietly forgotten. It feels like a continuous cycle, like a mouse on a wheel.

Over time, trust diminishes—not because love is gone, but because predictability is gone. And without predictability, the nervous system remains on edge.

People stay—but they stop opening up fully. Distrust became their daily portion. They start guarding their hearts, keeping their true thoughts and feelings hidden away. The relationship becomes a battlefield, with every interaction feeling like a potential landmine. Love without safety becomes a weapon, causing wounds that may never fully heal. In the absence of boundaries and consistency, the once vibrant connection begins to wither, leaving both parties feeling isolated and unfulfilled. In order to truly thrive, love must be a sanctuary, a place where vulnerability is met with understanding and care.

Boundaries prevent love from becoming emotionally unsafe.

Identity Erosion in Long Marriages

One of the most painful realities of boundaryless marriage emerges years later, when someone realizes how much of themselves, they have set aside.

They did not intend to disappear. They simply adapted—again and again—until adaptation became identity.

Dreams were deferred. Preferences were minimized. Opinions were softened. Eventually, the marriage functioned smoothly, but at the cost of one partner's internal vitality.

This is why some people feel lonely inside a long marriage.

Boundaries preserve identity without threatening covenant.

The Body Remembers What the Mouth Cannot Say

What is not spoken does not vanish—it relocates.

In many boundaryless relationships, the body begins to express what the voice was never allowed to articulate. Chronic fatigue. Anxiety. Irritability. Emotional numbness. Depression without a clear cause.

These symptoms are not random. They are signals.

The body carries the weight of unaddressed truth long before the mind gives permission to name it.

Boundaries interrupt this transfer of burden from soul to body.

What Children Learn Without Being Told

Boundary damage is rarely contained to the couple. Children absorb relational dynamics long before they understand them intellectually.

They learn what love looks like by watching how their parents relate. They observe who speaks freely and who stays quiet. Who adapts and who dominates? Who carries emotional responsibility, and who avoids it?

Later, these children may replicate familiar patterns—not because they want to, but because those patterns feel normal. As a result of having seen and heard it for themselves, they repeat the pattern in their own marriages.

Boundaries do not only protect marriages. They protect generations.

When limits aren't set, behavior patterns quietly pass from parent to child and are repeated from one generation to the next. What is modeled becomes normal, what is put up with becomes expected, and what isn't questioned is passed on, forming the next generation and the one after that. It's not just passed down through blood; it's also learned through familiarity, copying, and silence.

The Comfort of False Peace

One of the most deceptive consequences of missing boundaries is false peace. The relationship appears calm. Conflict is minimal. Life functions and continues as normal.

But beneath that calm is unresolved tension, unspoken grief, and emotional distance.

This fake peace hides the real problems that need to be fixed behind a front of unity. It makes people feel comfortable with the way things are instead of facing the difficulty of growth and change. Lack of limits actually keeps a cycle of dysfunction going, which makes it hard to feel truly connected and intimate in relationships. If there are no boundaries, there is no way to communicate honestly, understand each other, or heal and grow. At first, fake peace may seem like a good thing, but in the long run, it only keeps the dysfunction going and stops people from connecting with each other and being happy.

This kind of peace is fragile. It depends on continued silence. "How long can you stay quiet?" Until it blows up?

True peace is not the absence of conflict. It is the presence of honesty, safety, and mutual respect.

Boundaries disturb false peace in order to make real peace possible.

The Accumulation Effect

Boundary damage is cumulative. The harm from ignored, crossed, or weak boundaries doesn't happen all at once. Instead, it builds up over time, as repeated small violations lead to emotional exhaustion, loss of clarity, resentment, and a loss of trust or identity. Eventually, what was once manageable becomes heavy and unstable because of the steady buildup of damage rather than a single event that defines it. It rarely announces itself loudly. Instead, it builds quietly through repeated compromises and postponed conversations.

Then one day, something breaks.

A sudden numbness.
An emotional shutdown.
An outburst that feels disproportionate.
A desire to escape rather than engage.

People often say, "I don't know how we got here." But they arrived one unspoken boundary at a time.

A Necessary Clarification

Not every marriage without boundaries is abusive. But every marriage without boundaries is vulnerable.

Boundaries do not guarantee harmony. They prevent unnecessary harm.

They act as early-warning systems—interrupting patterns before damage becomes entrenched.

An Invitation, Not an Accusation

This chapter is not meant to shame the past. It is meant to illuminate the present.

If you recognize yourself here, the realization may feel heavy. That heaviness is not failure. It is awareness arriving at the moment you are strong enough to receive it.

Boundaries are not about what you failed to do before you knew better. They are about what you will no longer abandon now that you see clearly.

Reflection

As you reflect on this chapter, notice what resonates—not with shame, but with recognition. Where have you felt the quiet costs of silence, adaptation, or emotional fatigue?

Ask yourself: What has this relationship required of me that I never named as a cost?

Awareness is not condemnation. It is the beginning of restoration.

Prayer

God, who sees the hidden places, help me honor the truth of what I have carried. Heal what has been worn down by silence, and restore what has been diminished by unspoken compromise. Amen.

Summary

> Over time, small concessions that do not have any limits lead to internal confusion and mental survival instead of growing up.

People can use faith and endurance in a bad way to stop people from speaking the truth, which can cause emotional fracture. Not having any limits hurts safety and trust, making love feel risky and making people guard their hearts. People who are married for a long time may lose their sense of self, which can make them feel lonely. Also, children pick up on these unhealthy habits and use them in their own relationships later on. The chapter stresses that border damage builds up over time, which can make you feel emotionally drained and lost. Even though not all marriages with no rules are cruel, those who are in them are still at risk. The author supports knowledge as a way to heal, asking readers to think about the price of remaining silent and adapting in relationships.

THE DAMAGE BOUNDARIES ARE MEANT TO PREVENT

CHAPTER FOUR

Why Boundaries Are So Hard to Establish in Marriage

Why Clarity Feels Dangerous Before It Feels Healing

ONCE PEOPLE BEGIN TO UNDERSTAND the damage caused by missing boundaries, a painful question often follows close behind: If boundaries are so necessary, why didn't I establish them sooner?

That question is rarely asked with curiosity. It is usually asked with regret, guilt, or quiet self-reproach.

This chapter exists to answer it honestly—without excusing responsibility and without shaming the reader.

Boundaries are not hard because people are weak. They are hard because marriage reaches into the deepest places of identity, fear, faith, and belonging. It touches our need to be loved, accepted, chosen, and safe. And anything that threatens those needs will feel risky, even when it is right.

The Power of Hope in the Early Years

Most marriages begin with hope, not caution. People enter covenant believing the best about one another. They assume difficulties are temporary, rough edges will soften, and love will mature with time. They believe that people will change.

In that season, boundaries feel unnecessary. Behaviors that later become painful are often explained away as stress, immaturity, or adjustment. Hope whispers that patience will be rewarded, that growth is inevitable, and that things will settle.

And sometimes they do.

But sometimes they don't.

By the time patterns become clear, emotional investment is already deep. History has been built. Lives have intertwined. Walking things back no longer feels simple.

Boundaries feel much harder to establish once the cost of disruption becomes visible.

Faith That Becomes Conflicted

For many believers, boundaries are difficult not because they lack conviction, but because they have been taught a narrow version of faithfulness. Endurance is praised. Submission is emphasized. Forgiveness is elevated—often without equal attention to accountability, wisdom, or protection.

This creates internal conflict.

People wonder whether setting limits means they are being unloving or unspiritual. They worry that saying no might reflect a lack of grace or humility. They confuse Christlike sacrifice with continual self-neglect.

In this tension, boundaries feel like disobedience—even when they are necessary. Obedience is framed as yielding. So, it's seen as rebellious to say "no," question expectations, or limit access, even if those limits are healthy and needed.

Biblically, obedience is allegiance to God's will, questioning compliance with people. Jesus Himself routinely refused demands, withdrew from crowds, and set limits without sinning.

But faith was never meant to override discernment. Love was never meant to cancel wisdom. And covenant was never meant to silence conscience.

Fear of What Boundaries Might Cost

Boundaries threaten stability, even unhealthy stability. Most people want to feel stable, and they don't want to risk having the ground beneath them moved, even if it's unstable and slowly pulling them under like quicksand.

They raise uncomfortable questions: What if this creates conflict? What if things get worse? What if I am misunderstood? What if I am rejected? What if I lose the relationship altogether?

For many, it feels safer to tolerate what is familiar than to risk what is unknown.

Fear convinces people to endure patterns they would never recommend to someone else. It whispers that peace, however fragile, is better than disruption.

But what fear protects in the short term, it often destroys in the long term.

The Weight of Guilt

In many marriages, especially those involving empathetic or nurturing partners, guilt becomes a powerful barrier to boundaries.

One person learns to carry disproportionate emotional responsibility for the relationship. One person in the relationship ends up doing most of the emotional work, like dealing with feelings, keeping the peace, fixing issues, and keeping things together. The other person has a lot less to do. Over time, this makes things uneven and wears out the person who is carrying more.

They question their reactions. They minimize their needs. They worry about being "too much" or "too sensitive." When they consider setting limits, guilt speaks first.

Guilt says: You're overreacting.
Guilt says: You should be more patient.
Guilt says: Look at everything they do for you.

Over time, guilt replaces discernment.

Boundaries feel cruel not because they are wrong, but because guilt has been given too much authority.

Power Imbalances That Raise the Stakes

Not all marriages carry equal power. Power can come from personality, finances, education, spiritual authority, or emotional dominance. When power is uneven, boundaries feel especially dangerous.

The partner with less leverage may fear consequences—withdrawal, escalation, punishment, or emotional retaliation. They may have learned, consciously or not, that speaking up makes things worse.

In these marriages, boundary-setting is not merely uncomfortable. It is courageous.

And courage often emerges late—after exhaustion, numbness, or collapse. Emotional suppression is like sealing steam in a pressure vessel: it starts out quiet but gets steadily stronger until there is only one thing that can happen: the vessel breaks.

Trauma and the Habit of Adaptation

People shaped by early trauma often learned that safety came through accommodation. They became skilled at reading moods, anticipating reactions, and adjusting themselves to maintain peace.

In marriage, these patterns reappear automatically. The person does not think I should set a boundary. They think, How do I keep this from escalating?

Trauma trains people to adapt, not confront.

Boundaries require a sense of safety. Without it, survival instincts dominate. This is why some awaken only after years of quiet endurance.

The Shock of Waking Up Late

Perhaps one of the hardest aspects of boundary work is awakening late—realizing, years into a marriage, that something fundamental has been missing.

People feel disoriented. They wonder whether they have betrayed their spouse simply by becoming more honest. They worry that changing now is unfair, destabilizing, or selfish.

But awakening is not betrayal. It is clear when denial can no longer protect you.

Ephesians 5:4 (NKJV): *"Therefore He says, 'Awake, you who sleep, arise from the dead, and Christ will give you light.'"*

You cannot establish boundaries before you are able to see the need for them. And seeing often comes after capacity has grown. As capacity grows—through maturity, experience, or healing, they gain the clarity and strength required to see where boundaries are lacking and why they are necessary.

Boundaries Change the Relationship

This truth cannot be softened: boundaries alter relational dynamics.

They introduce honesty where there was silence. Accountability where there was accommodation. Equality where imbalance was normalized.

Some relationships grow stronger under this pressure. Others resist it. Some reveal limits that were always present but never named.

This uncertainty is why people delay boundaries. They fear what will be revealed.

But avoiding boundaries does not preserve the relationship. It preserves illusion.

Putting off setting boundaries causes more harm than good over time. As someone carries more than they should, it wears them down emotionally, makes them angry, and causes them to lose their identity and focus over time. Unspoken anger builds up until it comes out in the form of a heated argument. At the same time, unhealthy habits are reinforced and accepted as normal. When people aren't honest, trust falls, and growth is slowed for everyone because duty is never put back where it belongs. Putting up limits becomes harder and more disruptive the longer they are put off, which leads to more resistance and instability. What you avoid in the present doesn't go away; it comes back later at a much higher cost.

A Necessary Reframe

Boundaries are not a sign that a marriage has failed. Often, they are the first sign that someone has stopped abandoning themselves.

They are not evidence of hardness of heart. They are evidence of growth.

If boundaries feel difficult, it is not because you are wrong. It is because you are changing patterns that once kept the relationship stable—at a cost.

Reflection

Boundaries are often difficult not because they are wrong, but because they threaten what once kept us safe. Reflect on what made boundaries hard for you—fear, guilt, faith confusion, power imbalance, or learned patterns of adaptation.

Ask gently: What was I protecting when I avoided limits?

Compassion toward yourself is part of maturity.

Prayer

God of compassion, Meet me in the places where fear has shaped my choices. Replace guilt with clarity and confusion with wisdom that leads to life. Amen.

Summary

Setting limits in marriage can be challenging due to emotional investments, personal fears, and societal beliefs about endurance and love. Many individuals feel guilt for not establishing boundaries sooner, often ignoring negative behaviors until they escalate. A power imbalance in the relationship and past experiences of stress can further complicate boundary setting. The realization of the need for limits may come later, leading to confusion. However, creating boundaries fosters honesty and fairness in relationships, reflecting personal growth and a stronger sense of identity within the partnership. Emphasizing self-compassion is essential in overcoming barriers to setting limits.

CHAPTER FIVE

How to Set Boundaries Without Turning Love Into War

Clarity Without Conflict

For many people, the idea of setting boundaries immediately evokes confrontation. They imagine tense conversations, raised voices, ultimatums, or emotional fallout. This fear alone keeps boundaries theoretical rather than lived.

But healthy boundaries are not created through intensity.

They are created through clarity.

Setting boundaries is not about fixing your spouse. It is about telling the truth about yourself—calmly, consistently, and without apology for existing.

Boundaries Begin Inside, Not in Conversation

Before a boundary is brought up, it must be established inwardly, which means a person must first choose what they are accountable for, what they can accept, and what they are no longer prepared to carry. Without this internal resolution, boundaries tend to be expressed inconsistently, defensively, or with guilt, because the person is still debating with themselves rather than standing firm on conviction.

Many people try to set boundaries before they are clear about what they actually need, and the result is confusion, defensiveness, or retreat.

A boundary is not discovered in the heat of conflict. It is clarified in quiet honesty.

This often requires asking difficult questions: What situations leave me feeling diminished? What behaviors do I tolerate that quietly erode my peace? What have I normalized that actually violates my values?

Until these questions are answered privately, boundaries will sound uncertain publicly.

Clarity gives boundaries their strength!

The Difference Between Naming a Boundary and Attacking a Person

One of the most common mistakes in boundary-setting is framing limits as character critiques. When boundaries sound like accusations, they invite defensiveness rather than reflection.

There is a significant difference between saying, "You never listen to me," and saying, "I'm no longer willing to stay in conversations where my voice is dismissed."

The first assigns blame. The second claims responsibility.

Boundaries are most effective when they describe your participation, not your spouse's defects.

Speaking Without Threatening

Healthy boundaries do not rely on threats or emotional leverage. They are not delivered as warnings or bargaining tools. They are simply statements of reality.

A boundary might sound like this: "When conversations become disrespectful, I will step away and revisit them later."

There is no anger in that statement. No demand. No attempt to control. Just a clear description of what will happen going forward.

The power of a boundary does not come from how forcefully it is spoken, but from how faithfully it is lived.

Why Specificity Matters

Vague boundaries collapse under pressure. Statements like "Things need to change" or "I need more respect" are well-intentioned but ineffective. They leave too much room for interpretation.

Specificity removes confusion.

When expectations are clear, responsibility becomes visible. When responsibility is visible, patterns are harder to deny.

Boundaries do not need to be dramatic. They need to be understandable.

Timing and Tone Matter More Than Perfect Words

Many people wait to set boundaries until emotions overflow. By then, the boundary feels explosive rather than grounded. People often keep their uncomfortable feelings inside to avoid conflict, but someone can only take so much before they explode and do more damage when the angry words they've been holding in come out.

Boundaries are best introduced when the nervous system is calm. This does not guarantee agreement, but it increases the chance of clarity.

Tone matters because boundaries are not punishments. They are invitations to a healthier way of relating to your spouse. Even when they are resisted, they should be delivered without contempt.

Calm is not weakness. It is authority under control.

Expect Discomfort—and Do Not Misinterpret It

Setting boundaries almost always creates discomfort, especially in relationships where limits were previously absent. This discomfort is often misread as evidence that something is wrong.

But discomfort is not the same as damage. Damage indicates that the relationship has been damaged or cracked in a way that is difficult to repair. Even if efforts are made to repair and stabilize it, a scar frequently lingers as evidence of where trust and safety were previously jeopardized.

Change feels disruptive because it alters familiar patterns. When one person stops adapting, the system must recalibrate.

Discomfort means the boundary is being felt—not that it is incorrect.

Boundaries Are Not Negotiations

This is a subtle but crucial distinction.

Boundaries are not invitations to debate your worth, your needs, or your right to limits. They are not opening statements in a trial.

Once a boundary is stated, it does not require endless explanation. Over-explaining weakens resolve and invites negotiation where clarity is needed.

Boundaries are not arguments to win. They are truths to live by.

Marriage boundaries should result in a win-win situation for both partners, rather than a dynamic in which one person benefits at the expense of the other.

The Role of Consequences

Every real boundary carries a consequence—not as punishment, but as alignment. A boundary without consequence is a preference, not a limit.

Consequences simply describe what you will do to protect yourself if the boundary is crossed. They are not retaliatory. They are protective.

When consequences are lived consistently, boundaries stop being theoretical and begin to shape reality. When actions consistently match stated restrictions, people realize that the boundary is more than just an idea or a warning; it influences behavior and alters how the relationship functions in everyday life.

When Guilt Appears

Guilt almost always surfaces when boundaries are new—especially for those who have spent years prioritizing others over themselves.

This guilt does not mean you are wrong. It means you are breaking a familiar pattern.

Guilt fades when integrity is practiced consistently. Over time, self-respect replaces self-doubt.

A Gentle Truth

You do not need permission to protect your emotional, spiritual, or psychological well-being. Love does not require self-abandonment. Commitment does not require silence.

Boundaries are not acts of rebellion. They are acts of stewardship.

They are how love learns to stand upright instead of collapsing inward.

Reflection

Think about the boundaries you may need now—not as weapons, but as expressions of truth. Notice what clarity feels like in your body. Notice where you sense relief and where you feel resistance.

Ask yourself: What truth about myself am I ready to speak without accusation or apology?

Boundaries begin when honesty feels safer than silence.

Prayer

God of courage, Give me words that are grounded, calm, and true. Help me speak without attacking and stand without fear. Amen.

Summary

> Setting limits in marriage can be challenging due to emotional investments and fear of conflict, which often leads to feelings of sorrow and guilt. Due to their hope and faith in endurance, many couples fail to establish boundaries at first. Personal comfort, even in unhealthy forms, can feel safer than the uncertainty of confrontation. Power imbalances in relationships can exacerbate this difficulty, particularly for those with less power. The chapter

emphasizes that recognizing the need for boundaries may come later, leaving individuals feeling lost. Boundaries promote fairness and honesty, signifying personal growth rather than failure, and are crucial for maintaining identity within a partnership. Self-compassion and reflection on the barriers to setting limits are vital for development.

CHAPTER SIX

What Healthy Boundaries Sound Like in Real Life

Putting Words to Wisdom

ONE OF THE MOST COMMON questions people ask after understanding boundaries—and even after accepting the need to enforce them—is deceptively simple: "But what do I actually say?"

This question matters because boundaries do not exist only in the heart or the mind. They exist in words, tone, timing, and presence. Many people agree with the idea of boundaries yet struggle when it comes time to give them a voice. Not because they lack courage, but because they fear sounding unloving, harsh, unspiritual, or divisive.

Healthy boundaries are not delivered as ultimatums.

They are expressed as truth spoken with ownership and clarity.

The examples that follow are not scripts to memorize but rather displays of wisdom in language. They are meant to help readers recognize what boundaries sound like when they are rooted in love, dignity, and responsibility.

When Emotions Begin to Overwhelm the Relationship

Emotional boundaries are often the first to be violated—and the hardest to articulate. Many people stay in conversations long after they should have paused, not because resolution is happening, but because they fear disengaging will feel like rejection.

A healthy emotional boundary does not shut down connection. It protects it.

In real life, it may sound like this:

"I want to talk about this, but I'm feeling overwhelmed right now. I need a pause so I can stay present and honest."

Or:

"When the conversation turns accusatory, I shut down. I'm willing to continue, but not in this tone."

These statements do not attack the other person. They name an internal reality and set a condition for healthy engagement. They communicate willingness and limits.

When Time and Energy Are Being Drained

Many people violate their own boundaries with time and energy long before anyone else does. Saying yes becomes automatic. Rest feels selfish. Margin feels irresponsible.

But love that is always exhausted eventually becomes resentful. Love takes work, a desire to do it, and a choice. When love is constantly given without any breaks, limits, or ways to return the favor, it runs out. Because the person is giving from a place of emptiness instead of freedom, what starts as kindness slowly turns into duty, then weariness, and finally anger.

A healthy boundary around time does not require justification; it requires honesty.

It may sound like:

"I need time to think before committing. I'll get back to you tomorrow."

Or:

"I can't give this the attention it deserves right now. Saying no is the responsible choice."

These words honor reality. They resist urgency-driven decisions and protect the relationship from silent resentment.

When Forgiveness Is Confused With Immediate Trust

One of the most painful confusions in relationships, especially faith-based ones, is the belief that forgiveness must instantly restore trust and access.

This misunderstanding can lead to additional hurt and betrayal if the required limits and penalties are not established. Forgiveness is a time-consuming and effort-intensive process, and it does not guarantee that trust will be restored quickly. It is critical to communicate and set limits to protect oneself and the relationship from additional harm. Trust must be regained via continuous behaviors and responsibility. Without proper boundaries, forgiveness is readily abused, resulting in a cycle of hurt and shattered trust.

Healthy boundaries make a clear distinction.

In real life, this may sound like:

"I have forgiven you, but rebuilding trust will take time and consistency."

Or:

"I'm open to restoration, but I need to see change before things return to what they were."

This language reassures the other person that forgiveness is real, while also affirming that trust is rebuilt, not assumed.

When Family of Origin Begins to Intrude

Many conflicts in marriage are not between two people but between a marriage and external voices. External voices are the expectations, demands, and messages from outside the marriage that subtly influence how partners think, feel, and react to one another. When left unchecked, these voices overpower the couple's own ideals, transforming external influence into internal strife. What appears to be a marital problem is typically the marriage's resistance to voices that do not belong there.

Family influence, when unexamined, can quietly undermine unity.

A boundary here is not rejection—it is reordering priorities.

It may sound like:

"I value my family deeply, but decisions about our marriage need to stay between us."

Or:

"I'm not comfortable discussing this with others. Let's talk about it together first."

These statements honor family while protecting the sanctity of the marital space.

When Finances Become a Source of Tension or Control

Money is rarely just about money. It often reflects power, fear, or unspoken expectations.

A healthy financial boundary names responsibility without accusation.

It may sound like:

"I need transparency around our finances to feel safe and aligned."

Or:

"I'm not comfortable making this decision without discussion and agreement."

These words invite collaboration rather than control.

When Sexual Intimacy Requires Safety and Consent

Sexual boundaries are among the most sensitive—and most necessary. Obligation without dialogue slowly erodes intimacy.

A healthy sexual boundary is not rejection. It is protection of desire and trust.

It may sound like:

"I want intimacy, but I also need emotional safety."

Or:

"I'm not ready right now. Let's talk about what we're both feeling."

Such language honors both connection and consent.

When Faith Is Used to Avoid Necessary Conversations

Spiritual language can sometimes become a hiding place. Prayer replaces honesty. Faith replaces responsibility.

A healthy boundary here restores balance.

It may sound like:

"I believe in prayer, and I also believe we need to talk honestly about what's happening."

Or:

"Trusting God doesn't mean avoiding this conversation."

These words affirm faith while refusing spiritual bypassing.

A Final Word on Tone and Timing

Boundaries are not only about what is said, but also about how and when.

Healthy boundaries:

are calm rather than reactive

are clear rather than verbose

are consistent rather than emotional

invite responsibility rather than compliance

They are spoken with humility, not superiority.
With firmness, not fear.
With love, not guilt.

Learning this language takes practice. It may feel awkward at first, especially for those who were trained to prioritize peace over truth. But over time, these words become a bridge—between love and honesty, grace and wisdom.

Boundaries, when spoken well, do not push people away. They create the conditions where real connection can finally begin.

Reflection

Think about the limits you are being asked to articulate—not as pre-prepared statements, but as genuine reflections of your personal experience. Observe your internal response when you envision voicing them. Where does your body ease? Where does it become tense?

Focus on the areas where you have overextended yourself, overcommitted, or been deliberately ambiguous to maintain harmony. Observe the shifts that occur when precision supersedes elaboration and acceptance of responsibility replaces self-justification. Consider: What truth must I communicate with clarity and composure to preserve the integrity and authenticity of love? Healthy boundaries flourish when we speak the truth with respect, not trepidation.

Prayer

God of wisdom and truth,
Teach me to communicate with clarity. Help me to express what is true without being unkind, and to maintain my boundaries without feeling bad about it.
Grant me the courage to pause, the grace to be precise, and the steadiness to live by my words.
May my words foster connection, not fracture it, and may love be guided by honesty, not by silence.
Amen.

Summary

> Clear, calm, and honest communication in everyday situations is a sign of healthy limits. There are no demands or accusations here. Instead, these are statements of personal responsibility based on love, respect, and honesty. This summary shows with real-life examples how boundaries protect emotional ties, lessen tiredness and anger, tell the difference between forgiveness and trust, and keep the marriage safe from outside problems. It also talks about how important it is to set limits when it comes to time, money, closeness, and spiritual beliefs. It says that when limits are set in a humble and regular way, they do not break up relationships; instead, they create a foundation for more trust and real connection.

WHAT HEALTHY BOUNDARIES SOUND LIKE IN REAL LIFE

CHAPTER SEVEN

Enforcing Boundaries When They Are Tested

Holding the Line

SETTING A BOUNDARY IS AN act of clarity. Enforcing it is an act of courage.

Most people do not struggle to understand boundaries. They struggle to hold them when emotions rise, resistance appears, or guilt presses in. It is one thing to name a limit. It is another way to live it consistently when doing so feels uncomfortable.

This is where many people falter—not because they were wrong to set a boundary, but because they underestimated what enforcement would require of them.

Why Boundaries Are Tested

Boundaries disrupt familiar patterns. When a relationship has operated without limits for a long time, the introduction of clarity changes the rhythm of interaction. Roles shift. Expectations adjust. Access is regulated.

A spouse may test your boundaries by not respecting a request, asking for more than you can realistically give, or using guilt to sway your decision. This usually isn't out of spite—it can come from fear, insecurity, or simply being used to old ways of relating.

Testing is not always malicious. Sometimes it is unconscious. Sometimes it is confusion. Sometimes it is resistance. And sometimes it is an attempt—intentional or not—to see whether things will eventually return to the way they were.

Testing does not mean your boundary failed. It means it was noticed.

The Difference Between Explaining and Enforcing

When a boundary is first crossed, many people instinctively return to explanation. They clarify again. They rephrase. They add more context. They hope that if they just find the right words, their behavior will change.

But boundaries are not upheld by explanation alone. There comes a point where continuing to explain quietly undermines the boundary itself. Over-explaining turns limits into negotiations and signals uncertainty, even when none exists.

Enforcement does not require more words. It requires follow-through. Following through means standing firm when your boundary is tested. Be clear, kind, and consistent. Don't just speak the boundary—live it.

Trust God's wisdom and know that honoring healthy limits brings peace, not distance, to relationships.

What Enforcement Actually Looks Like

Enforcement is not dramatic. It is not loud. It does not involve ultimatums or emotional displays. It is often quiet and repetitive.

It looks like ending a conversation when disrespect begins.
It looks like stepping away rather than escalating.
It looks like it is no longer covering for behavior that has consequences.
It looks like changing access when trust has been violated.

Enforcement is simply alignment—your actions matching your stated limits.

Staying Calm When Emotions Rise

One of the hardest parts of enforcement is staying regulated when emotions are triggered. When a boundary is challenged, old fears often resurface: Am I being too harsh? Am I overreacting? Will this make things worse?

Calm is not indifference.
Calm is self-trust.

You do not need to defend your boundary every time it is tested. You need to live it.

Consistency communicates more than intensity ever could.

When Guilt Tries to Undo Progress

Guilt often appears after enforcement, especially for those who have spent years prioritizing harmony over honesty. Guilt whispers that you are being selfish, cold, or unloving. It suggests that maintaining peace should matter more than maintaining integrity. Setting boundaries isn't unloving—it's choosing honesty, respect, and emotional health.

However guilt does not always signal wrongdoing. Sometimes it signals growth.

Discomfort is expected when long-standing patterns change. Guilt fades when boundaries are practiced consistently and self-respect begins to replace self-doubt.

Recognizing Emotional Pushback

When boundaries are enforced, emotional pushback is common. This may include anger, withdrawal, silence, guilt-tripping, or accusations of being "different" or "uncaring."

These reactions are not proof that the boundary is wrong. They are often proof that the boundary is effective.

It is important not to mistake emotional discomfort in the relationship for relational damage. Growth often feels disruptive before it feels stabilizing.

The Line Between Discomfort and Harm

There is an important distinction that must be honored: discomfort is part of change; harm is not. Discomfort isn't danger; it's the stretch that leads to deeper trust and respect.

Boundaries may create tension, but they should never place you in danger—emotionally, psychologically, or physically. If enforcing a boundary leads to intimidation, threats, or escalating aggression, outside support is necessary.

Wisdom does not require isolation. Safety is never negotiable.

When Boundaries Are Repeatedly Ignored

If a boundary is clearly stated, consistently enforced, and repeatedly violated, the issue is no longer misunderstanding. It is resistance.

A spouse may resist boundaries by arguing, blaming, using guilt, ignoring your limits, or acting hurt. This often comes from fear of change or feeling like love is being withdrawn. But love and limits can go hand in hand—it's how trust and safety grow in a marriage.

At this stage, enforcement may require escalation—not as punishment, but as protection. Escalation might involve increased distance, mediated conversations, counseling with accountability, or temporary separation.

These steps are not failures. They are responses proportionate to what is happening. It doesn't mean the relationship is falling apart. It simply means you're responding in a way that matches what's really going on, with wisdom and self-respect.

Boundaries clarify reality. When reality resists clarity, stronger measures are sometimes necessary.

What Enforcement Reveals

How someone responds to enforced boundaries reveals far more than what they say.

Respect signals maturity.
Curiosity signals openness.
Defensiveness signals discomfort.
Contempt signals deeper issues.

Boundaries do not create character. They reveal it.

Boundaries alone don't make someone a better person. They protect you and guide relationships, but true character—like honesty, humility, and love—comes from the heart and a willingness to grow. Boundaries help, but they don't replace the need for inner change.

Choosing Integrity Over Illusion

Enforcing boundaries often means relinquishing the illusion that everything can remain the same while becoming healthier. Growth disrupts familiarity. Integrity disturbs false peace.

But the alternative—returning to silence, self-betrayal, and quiet resentment—is far more costly.

Enforcement is not about winning.
It is about living truthfully.

Reflection

Enforcement is where integrity is tested. Reflect on where you have stated limits but struggled to live them consistently.

Ask yourself: What am I afraid will happen if I follow through?

Fear loses its power when it is named.

Prayer

God of strength, Help me align my actions with my truth. Steady me when guilt rises and resolve wavers. Teach me that calm consistency is an act of love. Amen.

Summary

> Setting a boundary brings clarity but enforcing it takes courage. This chapter helps you recognize that resistance, especially from a spouse, is normal and not always harmful. Boundaries often disrupt old patterns, leading to emotional pushback like guilt

or anger. But holding firm, calmly and consistently, is a sign of growth, not failure. Enforcement isn't about punishing others—it's about living in truth, protecting peace, and trusting God. While discomfort is part of change, harm is never acceptable. When limits are repeatedly ignored, stronger steps may be needed to protect your well-being. Boundaries don't create character—they reveal it.

CHAPTER EIGHT

When Boundaries Were Never in Place

Late Awareness, Lasting Change: Repairing, Resetting, or Redefining the Relationship

THERE IS A PARTICULAR KIND of ache that comes with late awareness. It is not the pain of betrayal or sudden loss, but the quieter grief of realizing that something essential was missing for a long time—and that you did not have language for it then.

This kind of ache runs deep because it isn't tied to a single moment—it stretches across time. It's the sorrow of looking back and realizing your needs were never fully seen, your voice often silenced, or your emotions quietly dismissed. You may not have had the tools, the clarity, or even the permission to name what felt off. Now, with greater understanding, you see what was missing—but you can't go back and relive those years with that new wisdom. It's a grief that doesn't come with loud tears, but with quiet reflection—the ache of lost time, lost self, and lost connection.

People who arrive here often say, "If I had known earlier, things would have been different."

That thought carries weight. It brings sadness, regret, and sometimes anger toward oneself.

But awakening late is not failure. It is clear when you are finally strong enough to receive it.

When the Past Cannot Be Rewritten

One of the first temptations after awakening is to relitigate the past. People replay conversations, decisions, and seasons, wondering where things went wrong or what they should have done differently.

After awakening to what was missing, it's natural to want to go back and make sense of it all. Your mind replays old conversations, wondering what you missed, what you tolerated, and why you stayed silent. You might try to find the exact moment things went off track, as if solving the puzzle could undo the pain. But this constant mental rerun rarely brings peace—it only deepens regret. The past cannot be edited, and staying stuck there drains your energy, leaving little strength for the healing and rebuilding that needs to happen now.

This backward gaze rarely heals. It exhausts.

The past cannot be rewritten—but it can be understood. And understanding is not meant to trap you in regret. It is meant to inform you how you live now.

Boundaries are not retroactive. They are forward-facing.

Grieving What Was Lost—Without Staying There

Repair begins with grief. Not dramatic grief, but honest mourning for what was missing: unmet needs, silenced feelings, years spent adapting rather than living fully.

This grief does not mean the marriage was a lie. It means parts of you were not honored.

Allowing yourself to grieve does not weaken commitment. It strengthens clarity. Suppressed grief will always sabotage change.

But grief is a passage, not a destination. It must be felt—and then released.

The Reset Conversation

When boundaries are introduced late, a reset conversation becomes necessary. This conversation is not an indictment of the past, nor is it an ultimatum about the future. It is an acknowledgment that something must change if the relationship is to remain healthy.

A reset conversation sounds less like accusation and more like truth-telling:

"I'm realizing that I lived for a long time without boundaries. That has cost me—and us. Going forward, I need to live differently if this relationship is going to be healthy."

This kind of honesty may feel destabilizing. That is because it disrupts familiarity. But disruption is sometimes the doorway to repair. Humans are wired to cling to the familiar, even when it's unhealthy. There's a strange comfort in what we've always known—routines, roles, and rhythms that feel safe simply because they're predictable. We often stay in comfort zones not because they bring peace, but because they spare us from the fear of the unknown. Change feels risky; growth feels uncertain. So we settle, not out of joy, but out of habit—mistaking comfort for wholeness.

The Season of Recalibration

After a reset, the relationship often enters a season of recalibration. Old patterns no longer function, but new ones are not yet established. Awkwardness, tension, and uncertainty are common.

This season can feel unsettling, especially for couples accustomed to predictability. But recalibration is not regression. It is restructuring.

Patience matters here—not the patience of endurance, but the patience of intentional rebuilding.

When Repair Is Possible

Repair requires willingness from both partners. Not perfection, but openness. Curiosity. Accountability. A shared commitment to growth.

When both people engage honestly, late boundary work can actually deepen intimacy. Conversations become more real. Trust becomes more grounded. Respect grows.

Repair is slow, but it is possible.

When Reset Meets Resistance

Sometimes, however, reset is met with resistance. Boundaries are dismissed, mocked, or minimized. One partner longs for growth while the other longs for a return to what was familiar.

This is one of the most painful crossroads in boundary work.

The question becomes not "How do I fix this?" but "How do I remain honest without abandoning myself?"

In these moments, consistency matters more than persuasion. You do not undo boundaries because they are uncomfortable. You allow time and behavior to reveal whether growth is possible.

Redefining the Relationship

Redefining does not always mean ending the relationship. Sometimes it means adjusting expectations, changing access, or shifting the emotional weight you carry.

Ecclesiastes 4:9-12 NKJV *"Two are better than one, because they have a good reward for their labor. For if they fall, one will lift up his companion. But woe to him who is alone when he falls, For he has no one to help him up."*

Redefinition is not punishment. It is realism.

Some relationships heal fully. Others stabilize with limits. Some reveal incompatibilities that were always present but never named.

Boundaries clarify which path you are on.

Children and Late Boundary Work

When boundaries are introduced late, children may notice change. Conversations shift. Dynamics evolve. Tension may surface briefly.

But what children witness is not instability, it is modeling.

They see adults choosing honesty over silence and courage over avoidance. They learn that love does not require disappearance.

This is not harmful. It is formative.

Choosing Integrity Over Regret

You cannot change when you woke up. But you can choose how you live now.

Boundaries are not about correcting yesterday. They are about protecting tomorrow.

Living with integrity may feel risky at first, but it is the only path that restores dignity and peace.

Reflection

Late awareness carries grief. Take time to acknowledge what you wish had been different—without turning regret into self-punishment.

Ask yourself: What does integrity require of me now, not then?

You are not responsible for the past you did not understand.

Prayer

God of redemption, Help me grieve what was lost without living there. Guide me as I choose honesty over regret and dignity over denial. Amen.

Summary

> Realizing that boundaries were never in place can bring a quiet kind of grief—the sorrow of what was missing but never named. That awareness, though painful, is a sign of growth and a chance to move forward with clarity. Healing begins with honest grief, followed by a reset conversation rooted in truth, not blame. Rebuilding a relationship after long-standing patterns can feel awkward, but with patience and mutual commitment, deeper intimacy is possible. Even if change is met with resistance, staying consistent protects your integrity and helps define whether repair,

reset, or redefinition is needed for the relationship to remain healthy.

CHAPTER NINE

Love, Forgiveness, and the Courage to Set Limits

Love With Wisdom

FEW IDEAS CREATE MORE CONFUSION in marriage than love and forgiveness. They are sacred words—spoken often, prayed sincerely, and deeply woven into faith and covenant. And yet, they are frequently misunderstood in ways that quietly undermine dignity, safety, and truth.

Many spouses wrestle with questions they rarely voice aloud: If I forgive, shouldn't I move on? If I love, shouldn't I endure? If God forgives endlessly, who am I to set limits?

These questions are not rebellious. They are sincere. They are also incomplete.

Love and forgiveness are essential to marriage—but without boundaries, they are easily distorted into tools of self-erasure rather than pathways to restoration.

Forgiveness Heals the Heart, Not the Pattern

Forgiveness is an internal act. It releases resentment. It frees the heart from carrying emotional debt. It restores spiritual alignment.

But forgiveness does not automatically restore trust. And it does not automatically make a relationship safe.

Trust is rebuilt through consistency.
Access is restored through change.
Safety is created through accountability.

Many people forgive genuinely—and then feel confused when the same wounds reopen. They assume the problem is their inability to forgive fully, when in reality the problem is that forgiveness was never supported by boundaries.

Forgiveness alone isn't enough to stop unhealthy patterns from repeating. People often believe that if they truly forgive, things will get better—but healing a relationship also requires change. Without boundaries in place to protect what was forgiven, the same harmful behavior often returns, reopening emotional wounds. The confusion comes when someone believes their pain is a sign they didn't forgive "well enough," when in truth, what's missing isn't more forgiveness—it's the courage to say, "This can't keep happening." Forgiveness clears the heart; boundaries guard it moving forward.

Forgiveness addresses what happened.
Boundaries protect what happens next.

Grace Does Not Cancel Accountability

Grace explains behavior; it does not excuse harm.

Understanding someone's struggles may deepen compassion, but compassion does not require tolerating patterns that damage the relationship. When grace is offered without accountability, stagnation follows. Empathy replaces change. Intention replaces action.

Grace and accountability are not opposites. They are partners.

Grace says, "I understand."
Boundaries say, "This still cannot continue."
Together, they create the conditions for growth.

What Scripture Means When It Says Love "Endures All Things"

This is where many believers hesitate. Scripture tells us that love bears all things, believes all things, hopes all things, and endures all things. For some, these words have been interpreted as a call to limitless tolerance—to absorb harm silently, to remain indefinitely, to endure without protest.

But Scripture does not call love to endure destruction. Endurance in the biblical sense is not passive resignation. It is faithful perseverance in what is right. Love endures hardship, not deception. It endures seasons, not cycles of violation. It endures suffering for redemption—not for the preservation of dysfunction.

If "enduring all things" meant tolerating ongoing harm without truth or accountability, then love would contradict wisdom, justice, and truth—values Scripture upholds just as strongly.

Love does not endure the erosion of the image of God in a person.

What Love Bears—and What It Does Not

When Scripture says love bears all things, it speaks to posture, not permission.

Love bears weakness.
Love bears imperfection.
Love bears the slow work of growth.
But love does not bear abuse.
It does not bear chronic dishonesty.
It does not bear patterns that hollow out the soul.

Support without truth becomes enablement. And enablement is not love—it is fear disguised as faithfulness.

Forgiveness Is Not the Same as Relational Continuity

Scripture commands forgiveness without limit—but it never commands unconditional relational access.

God calls us to forgive freely, as an act of grace that releases bitterness and keeps our hearts aligned with Him. But Scripture never says we must keep ourselves in harmful, unsafe, or unhealthy relationships. Forgiveness is a personal, spiritual decision; access is a matter of wisdom and discernment. You can forgive someone completely and still choose to set boundaries, create distance, or require real change before reconnecting. Extending grace does not mean sacrificing your emotional, spiritual, or physical safety. Even Jesus forgave fully yet chose not to entrust Himself to those who were not trustworthy.

Forgiveness is always available.
Reconciliation is not automatic.

You can forgive fully and still require change.
You can release bitterness and still restrict access.
You can love sincerely and still say, "This cannot continue."

Even God forgives freely—and yet establishes boundaries, consequences, and conditions for restored fellowship.

Grace opens the door. Wisdom decides how—and whether—that door remains open.

Endurance Is Not Self-Erasure

Biblical endurance is never about disappearing. It is about remaining faithful to truth under pressure.

True endurance, as shown in Scripture, isn't about staying silent, shrinking back, or tolerating mistreatment. It means standing firm in what is right, even when it's hard. Godly endurance holds to truth, integrity, and righteousness in the face of resistance, not at the expense of your worth. It's not about erasing yourself to keep the peace—it's about walking in obedience, courage, and clarity, even when doing so feels costly. Disappearing to avoid conflict isn't endurance; remaining present with conviction and grace is.

Endurance without truth becomes endurance of harm. Endurance without boundaries becomes spiritualized self-abandonment.

Scripture never celebrates suffering that destroys dignity or silences conscience. Love that demands disappearance is not love rooted in God—it is love distorted by fear.

Jesus as the Model of Bounded Love

Jesus loved perfectly—and He lived with clear limits.

He withdrew from crowds.
He confronted misuse of power.
He refused manipulation.
He allowed people to walk away.
He did not entrust Himself to those who were unsafe.
His love was not passive. It was purposeful.

He endured the cross for redemption—not relationships that refused truth. Love without limits was never His model.

Love That Cannot Say No Is Not Love—It Is Fear

When people struggle to set boundaries, it is rarely because they love too much. More often, it is because they fear loss, conflict, or rejection.

Boundaries do not eliminate love.
They eliminate fear-based compliance.
Love rooted in fear shrinks.
Love rooted in truth grows.

A Redemptive Reframe

Setting boundaries does not mean loving less. It means loving honestly.

It says, "I care enough to tell the truth."
It says, "I value this relationship too much to pretend."
It says, "I refuse to let love become destructive."

Boundaries do not harden the heart. They protect it.

Where This Leads

When love, forgiveness, and boundaries are properly aligned, guilt loses its power. Faith becomes clearer. Decisions become steadier.

And when boundaries are still violated after all of this—after clarity, grace, and accountability—hard decisions may follow.

That is not failure.

That is discernment.

And that is where we turn next.

Reflection

Forgiveness may be familiar to you; boundaries may not. Reflect on how these two have interacted in your life.

Ask yourself: Where have I forgiven without protecting myself? Where might forgiveness need structure to remain healing?

Love matures when it is honest.

Prayer

God of grace and truth, Teach me to forgive without enabling harm. Help me love without fear and set limits without losing compassion. Amen.

Summary

> Love and forgiveness are central to marriage, but without boundaries, they can become harmful rather than healing. Forgiveness restores the heart, yet it does not automatically rebuild trust, ensure safety, or change destructive patterns. Scripture's call to endurance is not an invitation to tolerate harm, but to remain faithful to truth and dignity. Boundaries work alongside grace, not against it, creating space for accountability, growth, and real restoration. When love, forgiveness, and limits are properly aligned, fear loses its grip and discernment replaces guilt.

CHAPTER TEN

When Boundaries Are Violated and Hard Decisions Must Be Faced

When Words Fail and Reality Must Be Faced"

There comes a moment in boundary work when clarity alone is no longer enough.

You have spoken honestly. You have named limits without hostility. You have followed through calmly and consistently. And still, the same patterns return—sometimes softened by apology, sometimes hidden behind justification, sometimes defended with spiritual language or emotional pressure.

It is at this point that many people feel disoriented. They ask themselves whether they are being too rigid, too demanding, or too unforgiving. They wonder if persistence will eventually produce change, or if continuing to hope is simply another form of denial.

This chapter exists for that moment.

When a Violation Becomes a Pattern

Occasional missteps happen in every marriage. Growth is rarely linear. But there is a difference between struggling toward change and resisting it altogether.

When a boundary is violated once, it may indicate immaturity or oversight. When it is violated repeatedly—after clarity, after consequence, after conversation—it becomes communication.

Repeated violations say something words do not. They reveal how seriously your limits are taken. They show whether accountability is embraced or merely tolerated until pressure fades.

At this stage, the issue is no longer misunderstanding. It is a choice.

Having a choice means recognizing that continued boundary violations are no longer about misunderstanding; they reflect a pattern. You can't control someone else's behavior, but you can decide how you'll respond to it. It's the moment where you stop waiting for change and start choosing what honors your values, well-being, and dignity. Remaining silent or compliant is also a choice—one that often comes at the cost of self-respect. Choosing may look like setting firmer boundaries, seeking support, or stepping away—not to punish, but to protect what matters most: truth, safety, and peace.

The Subtle Erosion of Discernment

One of the most damaging effects of chronic boundary violation is the erosion of discernment. Over time, people begin to doubt their own clarity. They replay conversations, reexamine their tone, and search for ways they might have contributed to the problem.

Self-reflection is healthy. Self-erasure is not.

When you repeatedly question your right to limits in the face of consistent disregard, something important is being lost—not in the relationship, but within you.

Boundaries are meant to sharpen discernment, not exhaust it.

Manipulation Wears Many Faces

When boundaries begin to threaten familiar dynamics, resistance often becomes more sophisticated. It may no longer look like open defiance.

Instead, it takes subtler forms—guilt, minimization, deflection, or spiritual framing.

You may be told that you are too sensitive, that you are changing in a negative way, that you are making things harder than they need to be. You may be reminded of your faith, your vows, or your past mistakes in ways that quietly shift responsibility back onto you.

This is not growth. It is pressure.

The goal of manipulation is not resolution, it is exhaustion. It hopes you will grow tired of holding your ground and eventually return to silence.

Discernment means recognizing when conversation is no longer leading toward understanding but toward erosion.

Discernment is the wisdom to know when a conversation has stopped being productive and has started slowly wearing you down. It's realizing that no matter how calmly you speak or how clearly you explain, the other person isn't engaging with honesty or openness—they're deflecting, minimizing, or turning things back on you. Instead of building connection or clarity, these moments chip away at your confidence, your peace, and even your sense of reality. Discernment helps you step back—not to give up, but to guard your heart from emotional wear and spiritual confusion. It allows you to say, "This isn't helping," and shift your energy from trying to be heard to choosing what brings peace and truth.

Escalation Is Not Cruelty

There is a common belief that if boundaries are truly loving, they should not require escalation. This belief keeps many people trapped in cycles of explanation and disappointment.

Escalation means taking stronger steps when boundaries are continually ignored—like increasing distance or involving a spiritual counselor. It's not about punishment or anger; it's about protecting your well-being and honoring truth. Loving boundaries aren't passive—they respond wisely when words are no longer enough.

Escalation is not punishment. It is a proportionate response.

When a pattern persists, outside accountability or temporary separation may become necessary—not to threaten the relationship, but to protect what remains of your integrity.

Escalation acknowledges reality. It refuses to pretend that words alone can heal what behavior continues to damage.

The Difference Between Hope and Denial

Hope is rooted in evidence. Denial is rooted in intention.

Hope notices patterns of change, even when progress is slow. Denial clings to promises while ignoring repeated outcomes.

At some point, wisdom requires asking a difficult question: Am I hoping for who this person could become, or responding to who they are consistently choosing to be?

This question is not meant to harden the heart. It is meant to anchor it.

Who knows …it may encourage the individual to reflect on their resistance and serve as a wake-up call to support cooperation and compliance.

When Staying Requires Self-Abandonment

There is a line—quiet, often unspoken—where staying in a relationship begins to require the ongoing abandonment of self. When your voice must remain silent for peace to exist, when your limits must remain negotiable for harmony to continue, when your well-being is treated as optional, something essential has already been lost.

Covenant does not require self-destruction. Faithfulness does not demand disappearance.

A marriage that can only function when one person remains diminished is not being preserved, it is being sustained at an unacceptable cost.

Hard Decisions Are Not Hasty Decisions

Hard decisions should never be rushed, nor should they be endlessly postponed. They require time, support, prayer, and perspective. They are not reactions. They are conclusions formed through observation. To react is to make a decision prematurely, driven by discomfort or urgency, without pausing to examine repeated patterns, long-term impact, or underlying truth.

Choosing safety, distance, or redefining the relationship does not mean love has failed. It means truth has finally been honored.

Boundaries do not end marriages. They reveal whether a marriage can survive honestly.

Living Without Illusion

One of the quiet gifts of boundaries is that they remove illusion. They force clarity. They ask the relationship to stand on what is real rather than that for which is hoped.

This clarity can be painful—but it is also liberating. It ends the exhausting work of pretending. It restores dignity. It returns agency.

Whatever decision follows—repair, redefining, or separation is grounded in truth rather than fear.

A Word for the Crossroads

If you find yourself at this crossroads, hear this gently but firmly: you are not cruel for choosing safety, and you are not faithless for requiring change. You are not giving up because you reached a limit. You are honoring yourself because you finally see one.

Boundaries do not force decisions.
They make honest decisions unavoidable.

Reflection

If you are facing repeated violations, allow yourself to see patterns without minimizing them.

Ask yourself: Am I responding to who this person hopes to be—or who they consistently choose to be?

Truth is not cruel. It is clarifying.

Prayer

God of wisdom, Help me discern without hardening my heart. Give me courage to face reality without denial and peace in the decisions integrity requires. Amen.

Summary

When boundaries are consistently violated, love must be paired with truth, not denial. Repeated patterns of harm reveal a choice, not confusion, and call for courageous, sometimes escalating, action. Manipulation often replaces open resistance, wearing down clarity and confidence. Escalation—like seeking support or creating distance—is not unkind, but a wise and protective step when words no longer bring change. In the end, boundaries expose what's real and facing that reality allows for decisions rooted in integrity, not illusion.

CHAPTER ELEVEN

Discernment, Counsel, and the Wisdom of Not Walking Alone

Finding Clarity Through Community

BOUNDARY WORK CAN FEEL INTENSELY personal. It touches private pain, unspoken fears, and decisions that affect the most intimate parts of life. Because of this, many people try to carry it alone. They tell themselves they do not want to involve others, burden friends, or expose their marriage to scrutiny.

This instinct is understandable—and dangerous.

Boundaries were never meant to be navigated in isolation. Discernment sharpens in the presence of wise voices. Clarity steadies when it is witnessed. And courage grows when it is supported.

Why Discernment Needs Perspective

When you are inside a relationship, perspective is limited. When you're emotionally involved, it's harder to see clearly because your hopes, fears, history, and love all shape how you interpret what's happening. You might excuse harmful behavior, doubt your instincts, or overlook patterns because you're deeply connected to the person. Familiarity blurs red flags, and the desire for peace can silence your concerns. Emotions cloud judgment, making it difficult to separate truth from wishful thinking. That's why outside, trusted voices can often see what you can't.

Emotions, history, and hope all shape how reality is interpreted. This does not mean your perception is wrong, it means it is incomplete.

Discernment is the ability to see clearly without becoming reactive or rigid. That kind of clarity often requires someone outside the emotional system, someone who can hold the whole picture without being pulled into its intensity.

Wise counsel does not tell you what to do. It helps you to see what is actually happening.

The Danger of Isolation

Isolation amplifies confusion. When people try to carry boundary work alone, they often cycle between resolve and self-doubt. One day they feel certain; the next, they question everything. Guilt grows louder. Fear becomes persuasive.

In isolation, manipulation becomes harder to detect. Pressure feels heavier. Discernment grows tired. When you're isolated, there's no one to help you name what feels off. You may begin to question your instincts, justify harmful behavior, or believe you're overreacting. Manipulation thrives in silence—it confuses your thinking and wears down your confidence. Without wise support, it's easy to internalize blame or stay stuck in emotional fog.

Community brings perspective

Isolation allows distortion to feel like truth.

Support does not weaken boundaries. It stabilizes them.

Not All Advice Is Equal

This is where discernment matters deeply.

Advice that sounds caring is not always wise. Advice that sounds spiritual is not always grounded. Some counsel—well-intentioned though it may be—pressures people to endure harm, rush reconciliation, or silence truth for the sake of appearance.

Wise counsel does not minimize pain or maximize obligation. It asks careful questions. It honors complexity. It holds both covenant and dignity in view.

If counsel requires you to ignore your conscience, silence your voice, or abandon your well-being, it is not wisdom, it is pressure.

Choosing the Right Voices

The quality of counsel matters more than the quantity.

Healthy voices tend to share certain qualities. They respect boundaries in their own lives. They are not threatened by honesty. They value growth over comfort. They are able to listen without rushing to fix or judge.

Unhelpful voices often push toward extremes—either urging endurance without accountability or encouraging abrupt decisions without discernment.

The goal is not validation. The goal is clarity anchored in truth.

The Role of Professional Support

Some situations call for trained help. When patterns are entrenched, trauma is present, or communication repeatedly breaks down, professional support provides structure that personal relationships cannot.

Therapy is not a sign of failure. It is an investment in understanding yourself, of the relationship, and of the dynamics at play.

A skilled professional does not take sides. They help reveal patterns. They create space for accountability. They offer tools that transform insight into action.

Wisdom welcomes help.

Pastoral Care and Spiritual Covering

Spiritual guidance can be profoundly helpful when it honors both faith and reality. Healthy pastoral care affirms boundaries, resists manipulation, and supports truth-telling without coercion.

Unhealthy spiritual guidance, however, pressures silence, endurance without change, or premature reconciliation. It prioritizes appearance over health and peace over truth.

Spiritual authority is meant to protect conscience, not override it.

Accountability Changes the Dynamic

Accountability brings boundaries out of the private realm and into shared reality. It introduces follow-up, structure, and visibility.

When patterns are known and named, it becomes harder for cycles to continue unchecked. Accountability protects both partners—when it is grounded in fairness and clarity.

Boundaries strengthen when they are witnessed.

When Community Becomes Pressure

Community can heal—or it can harm.

When a community demands conformity rather than honesty, it becomes a barrier to growth. Statements like "Marriage is just hard" or "Everyone goes through this" may sound comforting but often function to silence necessary change.

A healthy community makes room for nuance. It honors process. It supports growth without rushing outcomes.

You need a community that encourages truth, not one that polices appearances.

Integrating Faith, Wisdom, and Reality

Discernment lives at the intersection of faith, wisdom, and lived experience. It refuses simplistic answers. It respects both spiritual conviction and emotional reality.

True wisdom does not ask you to choose between faith and self-respect. It weaves them together.

A Steadying Truth

You do not need everyone to understand your boundaries. You need a few wise voices who can help you stay grounded when doubt creeps in and pressure rises.

Boundaries grow best in safe soil.

Reflection

Consider who has been speaking into your journey—and who has not. Reflect on whether your support system encourages truth or pressures silence.

Ask yourself: Who helps me think clearly, not just feel obligated?

Wise counsel steadies the soul.

Prayer

God, who gives wisdom generously, Surround me with voices that honor truth and dignity. Protect me from counsel that confuses endurance with faithfulness. Amen.

Summary

> Trying to navigate boundaries alone often leads to confusion, guilt, and emotional exhaustion. Discernment sharpens when guided by wise, trustworthy voices who support truth, not pressure. Healthy counsel respects both your faith and your well-being, while harmful advice often pushes silence or premature reconciliation. The right kind of support, whether from friends, professionals, or spiritual leaders, doesn't take over your choices but helps you see reality more clearly. Walking with wise counsel brings stability, clarity, and the strength to honor both your dignity and your relationships.

CHAPTER TWELVE

Living With Boundaries:

Freedom, Peace, and a New Way of Relating

WHEN BOUNDARIES ARE FIRST INTRODUCED, they often feel disruptive. They disturb routines. They challenge assumptions. They ask relationships to adjust. But when boundaries are lived consistently—without drama, without apology, something quiet begins to emerge.

Life becomes calmer. Not because conflict disappears, but because confusion does.

The Quiet That Returns Inside

One of the first changes people notice after living with boundaries for a while is an internal quiet, they had forgotten was possible. The constant mental negotiation begins to fade. The endless internal questions—should I say something? Am I being too much? Should I just let this go?

Boundaries reduce the need for constant self-monitoring. When limits are clear, decisions become simpler. When consequences are consistent, anxiety loosens its grip.

Peace returns—not the fragile peace of avoidance, but the grounded peace of integrity.

Love Feels Lighter

Many people fear that boundaries will make them colder or less loving. What they discover instead is that love feels lighter when it is no longer carrying what boundaries should have held.

Resentment fades when expectations are clear. Generosity returns when it is no longer compulsory. Affection becomes genuine rather than dutiful.

Boundaries do not reduce love.

They remove the weight that was slowly suffocating it.

Intimacy Grows Where Safety Exists

True intimacy does not grow in environments where people must guard their words or hide their feelings. It grows where honesty is safe and differences are allowed.

When boundaries are respected, conversations become more real. Vulnerability no longer feels like a liability. Emotional connection deepens—not because conflict is absent, but because it is navigable.

Intimacy is not closeness without limits.
It is closeness. with trust.

The End of Emotional Over functioning

One of the most liberating outcomes of boundaries is the end of emotional over functioning. You no longer carry responsibility for regulating another adult's emotions. You stop anticipating reactions and managing outcomes.

Responsibility returns to where it belongs.

This shift does not make you indifferent. It makes you appropriately engaged.

You relate as a partner, not a caretaker.

Marriage Becomes a Choice Again

Perhaps the most profound change boundaries bring is this: marriage becomes something you choose, not something you endure.

You stay not because you are afraid, obligated, or silenced—but because there is respect, safety, and mutuality.

That choice renews covenant in a way endurance alone never could.

Not Every Relationship Looks the Same on the Other Side

This truth must be spoken gently and honestly: boundaries do not guarantee a particular outcome.

Some marriages heal deeply.
Some stabilize with clearer limits.
Some reveal incompatibilities that were long hidden.

Boundaries do not promise a specific result. They promise truth-based living. And truth, while sometimes costly, always restores dignity.

You Become Someone You Trust

Living with boundaries reshapes identity. People often describe feeling more grounded, more present, and more whole. They trust themselves again. They recognize their own voice.

They do not become harder.
They become clearer.

Clarity brings confidence. Confidence brings peace.

Faith Finds Its Balance

For people of faith, boundaries often restore spiritual health. God is no longer associated with guilt-driven endurance or silent suffering. Faith becomes aligned with wisdom, honesty, and responsibility.

Love and truth are no longer in competition.

Grace and accountability no longer feel opposed.

Faith becomes life-giving again.

The Strength Behind Honest Love

Boundaries are not about controlling others.
They are about stewarding yourself.

They do not weaken marriage.
They strengthen what is real and expose what is not.

They do not end love.
They make honest love possible.

The Beginning of Peace

If you have walked through these pages and recognized yourself, let this be clear: you are not late, selfish, faithless, or wrong for wanting peace. You are not broken for needing limits. You are not unloving for telling the truth.

Boundaries are not the end of the story.

They are the beginning of a life—and love—no longer lived at the expense of the self.

And that is not abandonment. That is wisdom.

Reflection

Imagine your life lived with clarity, not constant negotiation. Notice what feels lighter. Notice what feels possible.

Ask yourself: Who am I becoming as I live more honestly?

This is not the end—it is a beginning.

Prayer

God of peace, Thank you for restoring my voice and my footing. Help me live with boundaries that honor love, truth, and self-respect. May my relationships be shaped by honesty and grace. Amen.

Summary

> Living with boundaries brings a quiet peace that replaces confusion and emotional exhaustion with clarity and calm. Love feels lighter, intimacy deepens, and relationships become healthier when responsibility is shared and mutual respect is present. Boundaries don't limit connection—they make it safer, more honest, and more life-giving. Over time, they restore dignity, rebuild trust in yourself, and align your faith with wisdom and truth.

CHAPTER THIRTEEN

Where Boundaries Touch Real Life

The Places We Were Never Taught to Look

Most people think boundaries are only needed in moments of crisis. In reality, boundaries shape ordinary life. They govern how energy is spent, how love is expressed, how faith is lived, and how dignity is preserved. When boundaries are missing, life does not usually collapse quietly drains.

This section exists to help you see where boundaries matter most in everyday life and how their absence often explains the exhaustion, resentment, distance, and confusion that many couples feel but cannot name.

Emotional Life

When Compassion Slowly Turns into Absorption

Many marriages struggle not because love is absent, but because emotional responsibility is uneven. One partner becomes the primary emotional container—absorbing stress, anxiety, frustration, disappointment, and unresolved pain. Over time, emotional space narrows. Conversations become one-sided. The emotionally available partner begins to feel responsible for the emotional stability of the relationship.

This dynamic often looks like maturity. It can be praised as patience, empathy, or strength. But compassion without boundaries eventually becomes absorption. Instead of two adults processing life together, one person carries the emotional weight for both.

Emotional boundaries do not reduce care. They clarify responsibility. They recognize that support does not require self-erasure and that empathy does not mean emotional ownership of another adult's inner life.

Without emotional boundaries, love becomes heavy. With them, love becomes sustainable.

What This Looks Like in Real Life

One spouse comes home overwhelmed every day. They immediately unload their frustrations—about work, finances, family, and disappointments—while the other listens attentively, reassures, and absorbs. Over time, the listener stops sharing their own struggles because there is no space left.

They feel increasingly invisible, not because their partner is malicious, but because emotional responsibility slowly became one-sided.

What was missing was not love.
It was shared emotional ownership.

Communication

When Talking No Longer Feels Safe

Some couples communicate constantly and still feel misunderstood. Others avoid difficult conversations altogether, believing silence preserves peace. In both cases, boundaries around communication are missing.

Healthy communication boundaries protect how conversations happen. They draw lines around tone, timing, and respect. They acknowledge that not every moment is suitable for hard discussions and that raised voices, contempt, or dismissal are not acceptable forms of expression.

Boundaries here do not shut down dialogue—they make it possible. When communication lacks boundaries, people either escalate or withdraw. Neither leads to intimacy.

Respect is not optional in communication. It is the condition that allows truth to be spoken without fear.

What This Looks Like in Real Life

Whenever one partner raises a concern, the conversation quickly escalates. Voices rise. Accusations surface. Eventually, the other partner stops bringing things up—not because the issues disappeared, but because speaking feels unsafe.

Years later, distance replaces conflict. The marriage feels calm but hollow.

What was missing was not maturity.
It was permission to speak without fear.

Time and Energy
When Love Slowly Becomes Exhaustion

Many people live perpetually tired, not because life is unusually demanding, but because access to them is unlimited. Their time is always available. Their energy is always assumed. Their presence is always expected. In marriage, this often shows up quietly—one partner becoming endlessly accessible while the other rarely notices the cost.

Over time, availability replaces intention. Rest feels selfish. Saying no feels unloving. Even personal space carries guilt. The person giving the most begins to disappear internally, not because they lack devotion, but because they lack permission to pause.

Boundaries around time and energy are not about withholding love. They are about preserving the life that love depends on. Exhaustion does not deepen intimacy—it slowly erodes it.

Healthy boundaries honor the truth that time and energy are finite and that rest is essential, not optional.

What This Looks Like in Real Life

One spouse is always "on." They adjust schedules constantly. They respond immediately to needs. When they finally ask for time alone, it is met with confusion or subtle disappointment.

So they stop asking.

Fatigue becomes normal. Irritability increases. Joy fades. The relationship feels heavy, but no one can explain why.

What was missing was not devotion.
It was permission to rest without guilt.

Sexual Life
When Intimacy Loses Its Safety

Sexual intimacy in marriage is meant to be a place of connection, vulnerability, mutual desire, and trust. Yet for many couples, sexuality quietly becomes one of the most misunderstood and unprotected areas of life. Cultural expectations, religious assumptions, and unspoken obligations often replace honest dialogue. What should be a shared experience becomes something endured, avoided, or managed.

In many marriages, sex is framed primarily as duty. Desire is assumed. Consent is implied. Emotional readiness is rarely discussed. One partner's needs dominate while the other's discomfort remains unspoken. Over time, silence becomes the coping strategy—not because everything is well, but because talking feels too complicated or risky.

Boundaries in sexual life do not exist to restrict intimacy. They exist to protect it. They affirm that mutuality matters, that consent is ongoing, and that emotional safety is as important as physical closeness. Without these boundaries, sex may continue but trust slowly erodes.

Sexual boundaries also acknowledge that past experiences, trauma, fatigue, stress, and emotional disconnect all shape desire. Ignoring these realities in the name of obligation does not honor marriage, it damages it.

Healthy sexual boundaries create space for conversation without shame. They allow spouses to say, "This doesn't feel safe right now," or "I need to talk about what intimacy means for me," without fear of rejection or spiritual condemnation.

Intimacy cannot flourish where one person feels pressured to disappear.

What This Looks Like in Real Life

Physical intimacy continues in marriage, but one partner participates out of obligation rather than desire. They tell themselves that marriage requires it and that resistance would be unloving or sinful.

Conversations about discomfort feel awkward, so silence feels easier.

Over time, they feel disconnected—not just sexually, but emotionally. Trust weakens. What once felt unifying now feels lonely.

What was missing was not commitment or faithfulness. It was safety, consent, and honest dialogue.

Finances
When Money Becomes a Silent Burden

Money is rarely just about numbers. It represents security, power, trust, fear, control, and hope. Because of this, financial boundaries—or the lack of shaping the emotional climate of a marriage more than many couples realize.

In some marriages, one partner carries the full weight of financial responsibility. They manage bills, worry about debt, plan for the future, and absorb anxiety. The other partner may disengage, overspend, avoid conversations, or remain unaware of the emotional toll being carried.

Often, this imbalance develops quietly. Conversations about money feel tense, so they are postponed. Peace is preserved on the surface while anxiety grows underneath. Over time, resentment replaces partnership.

Financial boundaries are not about control or restriction. They are about shared stewardship. They ensure transparency, mutual accountability, and joint decision-making. Without them, one partner becomes the manager while the other becomes a dependent—or an adversary.

Money without boundaries turns into secrecy, fear, or power struggles. Money with boundaries becomes a shared responsibility rather than a quiet source of division.

Healthy financial boundaries also address expectations inherited from family or culture, how money was handled growing up, who had control, who carried fear, and who avoided responsibility.

What This Looks Like in Real Life

One spouse handles all the financial details, paying bills, managing debt, and worrying about the future. The other avoids discussions, spends without consultation, or minimizes concerns. When tension arises, it is dismissed to keep the peace.

Over time, anxiety grows. Trust weakens. Resentment settles in.

What was missing was not generosity or trust.
It was shared responsibility and honest engagemen

Family of Origin (Past)
When the Past Refuses to Stay in the Past

Many marital struggles are not created within the marriage itself, they are inherited. Family patterns learned in childhood shape expectations, communication styles, conflict resolution, and emotional roles. Without awareness, spouses unconsciously reenact what once felt normal.

Some people learned to keep peace by staying quiet. Others learned that control equals love. Some were raised to prioritize parents over partners, obedience over differentiation, and loyalty over honesty.

Boundaries with family of origin are often misunderstood as rejection. In reality, they are an act of maturity. Differentiation allows a new family unit to form without severing ties or dishonoring the past.

A marriage cannot thrive when childhood roles remain active and unexamined.

What This Looks Like in Real Life

Parents remain deeply involved in decisions. Expectations are heavy but unspoken. One spouse feels torn between honoring family and protecting the marriage. Conflict feels disloyal.

What was missing was not honor or respect. It was healthy separation and clarity.

Family of Origin (Present)

When the Past Quietly Governs the Present

Many of the people who struggle to set up in marriage have very little to do with their spouse—and everything to do with what was learned long before the marriage began. Family of origin shapes how conflict is handled, how emotions are expressed, how authority is perceived, and how love is earned or withheld.

Children adapt in order to survive emotionally. They learn when to speak, when to stay quiet, when to take responsibility, and when to disappear. These adaptations often become invisible scripts carried into adulthood. What once protected a child quietly governs the adult.

In marriage, these scripts are rarely questioned. A spouse who learned early that peace depended on silence may struggle to voice needs.

Another who grew up in chaos may normalize emotional volatility. Someone raised in a highly controlled home may confuse obedience with love or fear disagreement.

Boundaries with the family of origin are not acts of rejection. They are acts of differentiation—the ability to recognize where one person ends and another begins. Differentiation allows a new family unit to form without dishonoring the old one.

When family patterns remain unexamined, marriage becomes a reenactment rather than a new creation.

Boundaries here protect the marriage from being governed by ghosts of the past.

What This Looks Like in Real Life

One spouse feels intense guilt prioritizing the marriage over parents. Decisions are second-guessed. Parental opinions carry disproportionate weight. Conflict arises, not because the spouse does not love their partner, but because loyalty was trained long before love was chosen.

What was missing was not honor or gratitude.
It was permission to form a new primary bond.

Culture
When "Normal" Silences Conscience

Culture is powerful precisely because it feels invisible. It defines what is considered respectful, acceptable, shameful, or rebellious. Cultural norms shape expectations around gender roles, authority, endurance, emotional expression, and conflict—often without ever being named.

In some cultures, silence is a virtue.
In others, endurance is proof of character.
In many, questioning authority is equated with disrespect.

These norms do not disappear when people marry or migrate. They follow them into relationships, shaping behavior long after the environment has changed. When cultural norms conflict with personal conscience or emotional health, people often side with culture—not because it is right, but because it is familiar.

Boundaries challenge culture at the point where culture demands self-erasure.

This does not mean rejecting culture wholesale. It means discerning where culture aligns with life and where it contradicts dignity.

Culture explains behavior, but it does not define righteousness.

What This Looks Like in Real Life

A spouse remains silent during conflict because speaking up feels deeply wrong—even sinful. They endure patterns that harm them because suffering is praised and endurance is honored.

What was missing was not respect or humility.
It was permission to listen to conscience.

Spiritual Life

When Faith Is Used to Override Wisdom

Faith is meant to bring freedom, clarity, and alignment with truth. But when misunderstood, it becomes a reason to endure what should be addressed, to spiritualize what requires action, and to silence what needs voice.

Many believers are taught—implicitly or explicitly—that strong faith means fewer boundaries. Prayer replaces confrontation. Forgiveness replaces protection. Endurance replaces discernment. Spiritual language becomes a way to bypass responsibility.

But Scripture never presents faith as a substitute for wisdom.

Healthy spiritual boundaries recognize that prayer does not eliminate the need for truth, and faith does not cancel accountability. God does not ask people to override discernment to prove devotion.

When faith is used to silence truth, spirituality becomes heavy rather than life-giving.

Boundaries restore balance. They allow faith and responsibility to work together rather than compete.

What This Looks Like in Real Life

A spouse avoids difficult conversations by saying, "I'll pray about it." Years pass. The issue remains. Peace never arrives, only suppression.

What was missing was not faith or trust in God.
It was courage to align prayer with action.

Spiritual Altars and Generational Patterns
When Suffering Becomes Sacred

Some families, churches, and communities unconsciously build spiritual altars around suffering, silence, and endurance. These altars are reinforced through phrases that sound noble but quietly imprison lives:

"This is just how marriage is."
"We endure no matter what."
"God sees your sacrifice."

Over time, suffering becomes spiritualized. Pain is interpreted as virtue. Silence is mistaken for maturity. Endurance is elevated above truth. These altars do not usually announce themselves—they are inherited.

Generational patterns persist not because people choose them, but because they have never been named.

Boundaries are often the first act of altar-breaking in a family line. They interrupt cycles that have gone unquestioned for generations. This can feel disloyal, frightening, or spiritually dangerous—but it is often profoundly redemptive.

Breaking an altar does not dishonor faith.
It restores it to truth.

What This Looks Like in Real Life

A couple remains outwardly intact while inwardly fractured. They believe that staying silent protects God's reputation. Over time, dignity erodes and faith feels heavy.

What was missing was not devotion or loyalty to God. It was truth that sets free.

A Deep Integration

Family patterns, culture, spirituality, and generational altars are not side issues in boundary work—they are the soil in which boundaries either grow or wither. When these forces remain unexamined, people blame themselves for struggles that were shaped long before they had language to name them.

Boundaries do not erase heritage.

They redeem it.

They do not destroy faith.

They restore it to life.

Without boundaries, people inherit pain.

With boundaries, they interrupt it.

Reflection

As I think about where boundaries have been missing in my life, I notice how much I've carried without realizing it. Have I mistaken silence for peace? Have I called exhaustion love?

I'm learning that love isn't meant to cost me myself. In my marriage, in my faith, even in my daily decisions—where have I said "yes" out of fear, not freedom? Where have I stayed quiet to avoid conflict, but at the expense of my own voice?

What emotions rise in me when I consider setting boundaries around time, intimacy, or even with family? Do I feel guilty, selfish, or afraid?

I'm beginning to ask: who taught me what "normal" looks like? And is that "normal" still serving the person I'm becoming?

God, help me pause in these questions—not to shame myself, but to gently uncover the truth. Let me see what I inherited, what I've chosen, and what I'm now free to release. I don't have to carry what You never asked me to hold.

Let truth—not fear—guide what I rebuild.

Prayer

God of truth and grace,
Thank You for opening my eyes to the quiet places where boundaries were missing.
Help me recognize what I've carried that was never mine to hold.
Give me wisdom to honor my past without being governed by it.
Teach me to set boundaries that restore love, protect dignity, and align with Your heart for truth and freedom.
May I live with courage—not in reaction, but in faith-filled intention. Amen.

Summary

> Boundaries are not just for crisis—they shape everyday life, impacting emotions, communication, intimacy, and spiritual health. Without them, love turns to exhaustion, communication feels unsafe, and intimacy loses its connection. Many struggles in marriage stem from unexamined cultural, familial, and spiritual patterns that quietly shape how we relate. Boundaries do not reject these influences; they bring healing by allowing us to keep what's life-giving and release what's harmful. By embracing

boundaries, couples can move from silent survival to honest, life-giving connection.

APPENDIX A — A THEOLOGY DETOX

When Scripture Is Honored in Its Intention, Not Merely Quoted

This theology detox exists because many sincere believers were not harmed by rebellion, but by obedience shaped by partial interpretations of Scripture. The Word of God was honored yet often lived under pressure—without sufficient room for discernment, wisdom, and human reality.

Each section below follows the same pastoral rhythm:

Why this belief or verse is often misunderstood

How that misunderstanding forms in real believers

What Scripture actually intends

How the correction is lived out in real life

The goal is not correction alone, but restoration—so that love, faith, forgiveness, submission, and endurance can function as God designed them to: to give life, not diminish it.

1. "Love Bears All Things"
When Endurance Replaces Wisdom

"Love bears all things, believes all things, hopes all things, endures all things."
(1 Corinthians 13:7)

Why This Verse Is Often Misunderstood

This passage is frequently quoted to encourage perseverance in difficult relationships. Over time, it has been subtly transformed into a command to tolerate harm, silence truth, or remain indefinitely in destructive patterns—all in the name of love.

Many believers were taught that if love is real, it must endure anything.

Biblical Clarification

Paul is describing the character and posture of love, not removing the necessity of discernment, truth, or accountability. Scripture never presents love as blind or irresponsible.

Jesus loved perfectly, yet He:
confronted hypocrisy and sin (Matthew 23)
withdrew from unsafe situations (Luke 4:30)
refused to entrust Himself to those with wrong motives (John 2:24)
Biblical endurance is never detached from wisdom.

Lived Application

A spouse repeatedly endures hurtful words and dismissive behavior, believing that silence honors love. Over time, resentment grows and intimacy erodes.

Applied correction:

"I love you, and because I do, I can no longer continue this pattern without respect and change."

Love remains—but it is now anchored in truth.

2. Forgiveness
When Grace Is Confused With Access

"If your brother sins, rebuke him; and if he repents, forgive him." (Luke 17:3)

Why This Confusion Is Common
In many Christian environments, forgiveness is presented as the ultimate proof of spiritual maturity. As a result, believers feel pressured not only to forgive, but to immediately restore closeness, access, and trust, even when no change has occurred.

Any hesitation is often labeled bitterness or lack of grace.

Biblical Clarification
Forgiveness releases the debt of offense. Trust, however, is rebuilt through repentance and fruit. Even Jesus forgave freely while still requiring transformation.

Peter was forgiven, but restored through a process of truth, repentance, and recommissioning (John 21).

Lived Application
A spouse repeatedly apologizes for the same behavior but makes no lasting changes.

Applied correction:
"I forgive you sincerely. But for trust to be rebuilt, I need to see consistency and change over time."

Grace is honored without enabling harm.

3. Faith
When Trust in God Replaces Responsibility

"Faith by itself, if it does not have works, is dead." (James 2:17)

Why This Distortion Develops
Faith is sometimes taught as passivity: "Leave it to God," "Don't worry," "God will handle it." Without balance, these phrases become a spiritual way of avoiding difficult conversations, courageous decisions, or personal responsibility.

Biblical Clarification
Biblical faith activates responsibility; it never cancels it.
Nehemiah prayed and built walls.
Jesus trusted the Father and confronted truth.
Faith works alongside wisdom and action.

Lived Application
A couple avoids discussing finances, saying, "God will provide."

Applied correction:
"We trust God, and because we do, we need to steward our resources with honesty and wisdom."

Faith becomes active, not evasive.

4. Submission
When Silence Is Spiritualized

"Submit to one another out of reverence for Christ." (Ephesians 5:21)

Why This Teaching Has Caused Pain
In some contexts, submission has been reduced to silence, endurance, and self-erasure—especially for women, but also for men in imbalanced relationships. Speaking up is framed as rebellion rather than responsibility.

Biblical Clarification
Biblical submission is voluntary, mutual, and rooted in trust. Jesus submitted to the Father while still speaking truth, setting limits, and confronting injustice.

Submission never requires the loss of voice or dignity.

Lived Application
A wife remains silent about emotional neglect, believing submission requires endurance.

Applied correction:
"I honor you, and because I do, I need to speak honestly about what I'm experiencing."

Submission and truth are no longer in conflict.

5. Headship and Authority
When Leadership Loses Its Guardrails

"Husbands, love your wives, just as Christ loved the church and gave Himself up for her."(Ephesians 5:25)

Why This Misunderstanding Persists
Headship is often associated with decision-making power, privilege, or final authority—while the biblical emphasis on self-sacrifice, restraint, and accountability is overlooked.

Biblical Clarification
Christ leads through self-giving love, not domination. In Scripture, greater authority always carries greater responsibility, not unlimited access. Boundaries do not oppose headship; they protect it from distortion.

Lived Application
A husband makes unilateral decisions, invoking his role as head.

Applied correction:
"My role means I must listen, protect, and consider how my decisions affect our relationship." Leadership is strengthened through accountability.

6. Suffering
When All Pain Is Automatically Labeled Redemptive "And we know that in all things God works for the good of those who love Him...

"(Romans 8:28)

Why This Interpretation Is Tempting
Because Scripture acknowledges suffering, many believers assume all pain must be endured for spiritual growth. This can lead to the spiritualization of destructive cycles that produce no fruit.

Biblical Clarification
God can redeem suffering, but He does not glorify unnecessary or repetitive pain without transformation. Jesus healed suffering; He did not institutionalize it.

Lived Application
A couple remains stuck in the same conflicts for years, saying, "God is teaching us something."

Applied correction:
"If nothing is changing, this is not growth. Seeking help is an act of wisdom." Redemption includes transformation.

7. "Protecting the Name of Christ"

When Image Replaces Truth

"Then you will know the truth, and the truth will set you free." (John 8:32)

Why Silence Feels Faithful

Many believers fear that acknowledging struggles will dishonor God or damage their witness. Silence becomes a misguided form of loyalty.

Biblical Clarification

Throughout Scripture, God is honored by truth, integrity, and justice, not by appearances. Religious façades are consistently confronted by Jesus.

Lived Application

A leader hides marital dysfunction to protect ministry image.

Applied correction:

"Seeking help honors God more than maintaining a façade." Integrity replaces fear.

Final Detox Declaration

Boundaries do not weaken faith.
They make it livable.
Truth does not destroy love.
It protects it.
Wisdom does not cancel obedience.
It completes it.

APPENDIX A — A THEOLOGY DETOX

CONCLUSION

Living Whole, Loving Well

Reaching the end of this book does not mean the work is finished, it means a new kind of awareness has begun.

If you have walked carefully through these chapters, you may now see relationships, faith, and even Scripture differently. You may recognize patterns you once excused, beliefs you once carried unquestioned, or pains you once assumed were required. This awareness is not a sign of spiritual failure; it is often the beginning of spiritual maturity.

Boundaries do not oppose love.
They protect it from distortion.
They do not weaken faith.
They give it structure and sustainability.
They do not cancel forgiveness.
They preserve truth, dignity, and responsibility.

The Theology Detox may have challenged ideas that once felt sacred simply because they were familiar. But detoxification is not destruction, it is restoration. It removes what has accumulated and obstructed life so that what is essential can flow freely again.

You were never called to endure endlessly without wisdom. You were never asked to remain silent at the expense of truth. You were never commanded to sacrifice your God-given identity to prove faithfulness.

Healthy boundaries invite you into a better way of loving—one where grace and truth walk together, where forgiveness is sincere but not careless, and where commitment is rooted in responsibility rather than fear.

As you move forward, you may find that setting boundaries feels uncomfortable at first. That is often because you are breaking patterns that once defined you. But over time, clarity replaces confusion, peace replaces resentment, and love becomes lighter—not because it is weaker, but because it is finally aligned.

May your relationships be marked by honesty and respect. May your faith be grounded in truth and wisdom. And may your life reflect the wholeness God intended from the beginning.

You were created to love well.
You were called to live whole.
And you were never meant to lose yourself in the process.

AUTHOR BIO

Dr. Jean Héder Petit-Frère is a pastor, apostolic leader, teacher, and author with almost 40 years of ministry experience. He is known for his clear, compassionate, kingdom based and Bible-centered approach to faith, relationships, and personal growth.

As the founder of Shabach Ministries International, a faith-based, not-for-profit ministry, he serves churches, families, and leaders across cultures and nations. His apostolic work focuses on strengthening foundations, restoring balance, and equipping leaders to serve with wisdom, dignity, and spiritual maturity.

He is also the visionary behind the Kingdom Leadership Institute, where he equips emerging and established leaders to serve with integrity, clarity, and purpose.

Boundaries That Heal reflects both his pastoral journey and his apostolic commitment to aligning love, faith, and truth for healthy, life-giving relationships.

www.ingramcontent.com/pod-product-compliance
Lightning Source LLC
Chambersburg PA
CBHW052144070526
44585CB00017B/1967